Complete Text

Frederick Noad
First Book for the Guitar

GUI TAR

Illustrations by Charles Boyer

ED-3461

ISBN 0-7935-5522-1

G. SCHIRMER, Inc.

DISTRIBUTED BY

 HAL•LEONARD™
CORPORATION

7777 W. BLUEMOUND RD. P.O. BOX 13819 MILWAUKEE, WI 53213

Reg. 48599c

About The Author

Frederick Noad, the author of a number of widely used educational guitar books and anthologies, was born in Belgium. Educated in England, he is a graduate of Oxford University.

Originally trained in the violin and piano, Noad took up the guitar in his early teens, and was later a performing member in master classes of Andres Segovia and Julian Bream.

After coming to the United States in 1957 he founded the "Spanish Guitar Center" in Hollywood, modeled on a similar teaching establishment in London, which he directed until 1965. During this period he studied composition with Mario Castelnuovo-Tedesco at the latter's home in Beverly Hills.

In 1966 Noad launched the series "Playing the Guitar" for educational television. The programs were enthusiastically received from coast to coast, and are credited with introducing 100,000 new players to the instrument.

Noad has been a faculty member of the University of California, Irvine, and the California Institute of the Arts. He performs as a soloist, as part of a duet team, in concert with a lyric tenor and also as a continuo player in early opera. In addition to the guitar he plays the lute and theorbo.

Part One

CONTENTS

TO THE READER

This book makes three assumptions. The first is that you have just acquired a guitar and are ready for the pleasure and challenge of beginning to play. The second is that you know absolutely nothing about music or how it is written. The third is that you know nothing about the guitar itself.

Obviously if you *do* know something already you have an advantage, and this will help you through the early stages: But even so it will be a good idea to go carefully through the checklists provided to be absolutely sure that you have not missed some fundamental point.

For best results with this method, the secret is to go one step at a time, not trying to do too much at one sitting, and particularly not trying to jump ahead to the more difficult material.

Progression by simple stages is the key to major achievement. There is a saying in the East that a journey of a thousand miles begins with a single step; and the designers of do-it-yourself kits, from ham radios to harpsichords, have found that a person of average ability can construct amazingly complex finished items by following a clear progression of instructions. However, just as the omission of one part from an electronic kit can mean disaster, so in learning music the skipping of steps can mean failure to form the groundwork on which future progress depends.

This book is a practical manual; so as information is given, there is an action required to reinforce the memory. If the action involves saying something out loud, for instance when counting, do it without feeling foolish. As with names, verbal repetition is a strong aid to memorization.

If you possibly can, go to a teacher. Many of the musical exercises are designed for the teacher to play with the student, and they sound fuller and more interesting played this way. Also, your overall progress will be speeded up by the help that a good teacher can give you. But if access to a teacher is impossible, you can still achieve wonders if you remember that you must be the teacher as well as the student and impose on yourself a systematic and self-critical approach.

The main purpose is enjoyment. With the right start you can look forward to many years of pleasure and satisfaction. Learning to read music is not nearly as difficult as most people think, and with the correct approach it is well within the capabilities of the average seven year old child. The music symbols are not academic dogma; they are a tool for you to use to achieve your goals. You are the master, and they represent the servant that assists you on your musical journey.

The physical movements involved in playing music are known as "technique." Some beginning books leave this to the teacher and concentrate on musical notation only. This book attempts to give you the clearest possible explanation of how to perform the important basic movements in case a teacher is not available. Habits must be formed for the movements to become automatic, and it is as easy to form good habits as bad ones. But bad habits are hard to lose, so particular care in the first stages will save much time in the future.

Good luck, and welcome to the world of the guitar.

NOTE TO THE TEACHER

As far as possible I have tried to make this first approach to the guitar an enjoyable experience for both student and teacher. The exercises are in the form of duets, so that even the most basic process of note-learning can be fun. This usually comes as a surprise to the student who does not expect to be participating in "real music" at such an early stage, and his delight in his achievement serves as an incentive to both parties.

The scope of Part One has been carefully defined to include a fully illustrated description of all major techniques, the complete notes of the first position including accidentals, and the fundamentals of music up to the eighth note. The more advanced subjects, such as the dotted quarter note, theory of keys and scales, and notes faster than the eighth note, have been reserved for Part Two. Part Three completes the basic knowledge appropriate to the first year of study.

ABOUT THE GUITAR

This book is about the nylon-strung guitar of the type shown in the illustration. It is known variously as the classical (or classic) guitar, the concert guitar, or the finger-style guitar to distinguish it from other types with steel strings which are sometimes amplified electrically.

The classical guitar needs no amplification since of all the types it has the greatest natural resonance, and when professionally played can be clearly heard in a full-sized auditorium.

The same musical notation is shared by all forms of the instrument, but electric guitars are usually played with a plectrum of plastic or tortoise shell whereas the nylon-strung guitar is played with the fingers (or fingernails as we shall shortly see).

NAMING THE PARTS

For future reference it is important to know the correct name for the various parts of the guitar. After studying the diagram (Fig. 1), identify each of the following on your own instrument.

Fig. 1 THE ANATOMY OF THE CLASSICAL GUITAR.

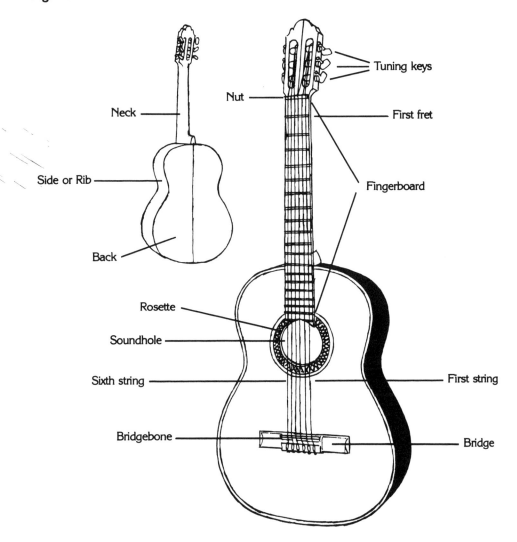

Of particular importance is the numbering of the strings. Remember that the first string is the thinnest, highest in pitch, and closest to the floor when you are sitting in the normal playing position.

HOW GUITAR MUSIC IS WRITTEN

The following section explains all the musical symbols used in this book. The purpose is to give you an overall picture and a general section for reference; however, each item is introduced and practiced in the lessons which follow so as to build up the real familiarity that comes with use.

Music for the guitar is written on what is known as a STAFF, consisting of five horizontal lines. Each line and each space between represents a musical sound, lower sounds at the bottom of the staff and higher at the top.

At the beginning of each staff is a CLEF sign. The sign illustrated is always used for the guitar, and is known as a TREBLE or G CLEF (since it curls around the line that represents the note G). Other instruments of higher or lower pitch use different clefs, which indicate the set of notes more commonly used by that instrument.

Clef Sign →

The Musical Staff

The notes represented by the treble clef are as follows:

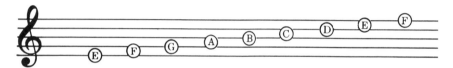

For memorization purposes they are usually divided into two sets:

the lines   and the spaces

Obviously the nine lines and spaces are not enough for all the notes, so extra lines are drawn above and below the staff where necessary

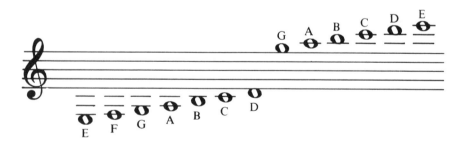

The extra lines are known as ledger lines. Notice that only the letters A to G are used for naming notes; after G the progression starts again with another A. You will soon find out in practice the similiarity between one A and the next one eight notes (an OCTAVE) higher or lower. Your ear will tell you that although one is higher in pitch than the other they have a similiarity in sound.

Now here are the six strings of the guitar expressed in notation.

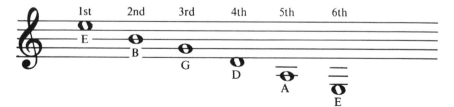

NOTES AND RESTS

The symbols drawn on a line or space indicate how long each note is to last. Periods of silence are known as RESTS, and each note has an equivalent rest sign. Measurement is by even counts, also known as beats from the expression "beating time," which is what a conductor does with his baton.

The table below shows the note lengths in beats when each beat lasts a quarter note (the commonest time you will encounter).

SYMBOL	NAME	EQUIVALENT REST	DURATION
𝅝	Whole Note (Semibreve)	▬	Four Beats
𝅗𝅥·	Dotted Half Note (Dotted Minim)	▬·	Three Beats
𝅗𝅥	Half Note (Minim)	▬	Two Beats
𝅘𝅥	Quarter Note (Crochet)	𝄽	One Beat
𝅘𝅥𝅮	Eighth Note (Quaver)	𝄾	Half a Beat

The names given are those used in the United States. The names in brackets are those in common usage in England.

A dot increases any note by half its value again. Hence a dotted quarter note lasts one and a half beats, as discussed later.

Two or more eighth notes may be joined together thus: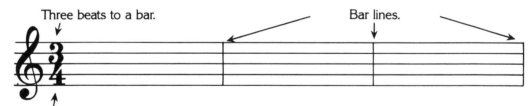

The line joining them is known as a BEAM. The thin upright line is a STEM.

To assist counting and rhythm music is divided into BARS or MEASURES of a given number of counts. Bar lines are drawn vertically as shown below. At the beginning of every piece a TIME SIGNATURE shows how many beats there are in each bar, and also how long each beat lasts. The *upper* number tells you how many beats are in each bar, the *lower* number the duration of each beat.

Three beats to a bar.   Bar lines.

Each beat lasts a quarter note.

Much of the above may seem difficult to grasp in theory, but it will become clear as you start to play from the music. It is necessary to list this rather large number of theoretical points because even the first and easiest piece of music must contain a staff, clef sign, time signature, etc. However, a basic concept will do at this point if you remember that this section is here for reference.

Now here is a checklist to see how many of the points you already remember.

1. Which letters are used for musical notes?

2. Which notes are represented by the lines of the staff? Which by the spaces?

3. How many beats does a half note last? A dotted half note?

4. Why are clef signs used?

5. What is a time signature? Which number indicates how many beats there are in a bar?

6. What are bar lines? Why are they used?

TUNING

Fig. 2 ATTACHING THE STRINGS
TO THE BRIDGE.

Fig. 3 ATTACHING THE STRINGS
TO THE TUNING KEYS.

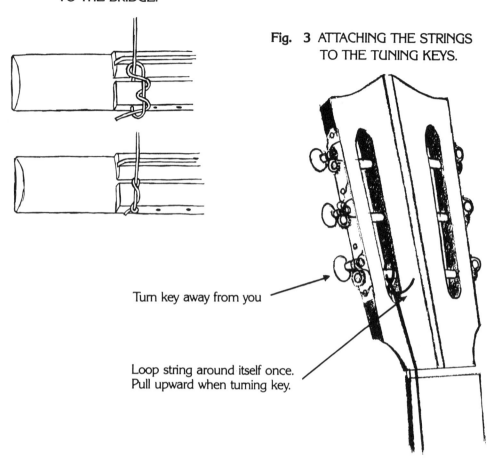

Turn key away from you

Loop string around itself once.
Pull upward when tuning key.

With the strings correctly tied as shown above, the easiest way to tune in the early stages is to align the strings with the same notes on a piano. The diagram shows which notes to use.

Fig. 4 THE RELATIONSHIP OF GUITAR TUNING TO NOTES ON THE PIANO.

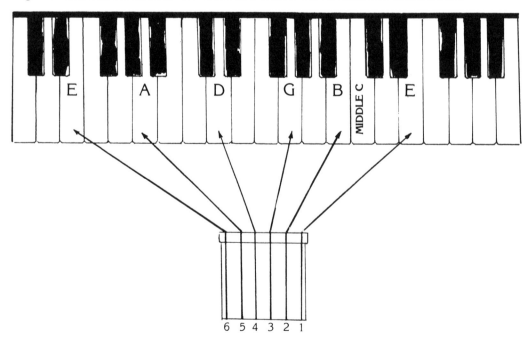

The tuning keys are used to tighten or loosen each string until it sounds the same as the given note on the piano. At first it is hard to hear if two notes are *exactly* in tune, but this comes with practice.

Begin by tuning the strings as closely as possible to the piano, then check them off in the steps given below.

1. Play the 6th string with a left hand finger behind the 5th fret. The note should be the same as the 5th string played open (i.e. with no left hand finger on it). If it is not the same, adjust the 5th string (*not* the 6th).

2. Now play the 5th string at the 5th fret. It should be the same as the 4th string open. If not, adjust the *4th* string.

3. Follow the same steps, playing the 4th string at the 5th fret to obtain the sound for the 3rd string open. Adjust the 3rd string if necessary.

4. Now there is a slight change in procedure. The 3rd string must be played at the *4th* fret (not the 5th) to give the same sound as the 2nd string. Adjust the 2nd string if necessary.

5. Finally play the 2nd string at the 5th fret to obtain the sound for the 1st string.

The above procedure is known as *relative* tuning, each string being tuned in relation to its neighbor. When the relationships are understood and have been practiced a few times, it only becomes necessary to have the pitch for one string, since the others can be tuned to it.

If a piano is not available, all music stores can provide either a pitch pipe or tuning fork to help you establish a correct pitch.

Of the two, the pitch pipe is easier to handle since it can be sounded while held in the mouth thereby leaving both hands free to play and adjust the tuning. A vibrating tuning fork must be held with the handle touching a resonant surface to be properly heard, and this ties up one of the hands. However, the tuning fork has the advantage of greater accuracy.

SPECIAL TUNING TIPS

1. A very small turn of the tuning key may not be sufficient to change the pitch of the string, due to play in the mechanism. A reasonably positive movement must be made.

2. If a string is minutely high in pitch, it may be brought down the necessary fraction by stretching it with the right hand. This is done by taking hold of the string and giving it a twist as if turning a handle.

3. The stretching procedure described above is particularly useful in taking the slack out of new strings. Otherwise new strings have to be constantly tuned since they keep going down when played. Beginners often think that this is because the strings are slipping, but if they are correctly tied as shown in the diagrams no slippage will occur.

If you still have problems after working through the above steps, do not hesitate to seek the help of a musical friend or a music shop. The staff at any shop where guitars are sold is accustomed to helping beginners, and a live demonstration can be most helpful. Now, as a quick check before continuing, answer the following questions.

1. What is an open string?

2. What is relative tuning?

3. Which string must be sounded at the 4th fret to give the pitch for its neighbor above?

4. How may a string be lowered in pitch without using the tuning key?

5. Why do new strings need to be stretched?

BEGINNING TO PLAY

Fig. 5 THE PLAYING POSITION

THE PLAYING POSITION

Study the diagram, and try to take a position as close to it as possible. The following points are important.

1. Sit on the *front* of the chair. The position involves leaning forward slightly, which is more difficult if you sit back in the chair.

2. Be sure to use a footstool or something similar to raise your left leg. This is the main support point for the guitar.

3. Take the weight of your right forearm on the guitar. Don't curl the arm around the guitar, since this will throw the right hand into the wrong position.

4. When you need to look at the front of the guitar, move your head forward rather than tilting the guitar back to you. This way you maintain control and domination of the instrument.

THE RIGHT HAND

Now look at the right hand in the diagram. Notice that the knuckles are aligned with the strings. If you can remember this one point, you will be well on the way to establishing a good right hand position. The wrist should be arched up from the face of the guitar, and should *never* touch it.

THE REST STROKE

Fig. 6 THE REST-STROKE.

A. Preparation: Notice the angle of the finger.

B. The detail shows the nail in relation to the string

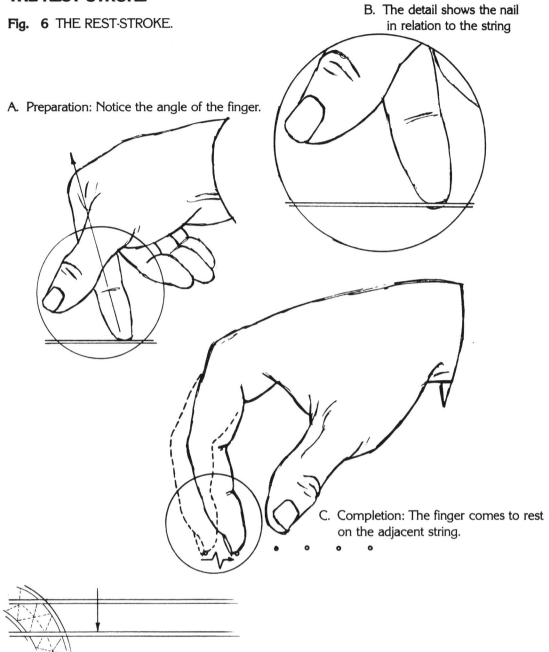

C. Completion: The finger comes to rest on the adjacent string.

D. For the strongest sound the nail pulls directly across to the adjacent string.

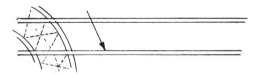

E. For better tone quality the nail travels in the direction shown.

Preparation

Place the tip of the index finger on the first string, so that the fingertip is in contact with it, with the nail projecting over the string. The left-hand edge of the nail (as you look down on your hand) is in contact with the string.

Completion

Draw the finger towards the second string. Your nail first pulls against the original string, then releases it to play the note. The fingertip comes to *rest* on the second string, giving the movement its name; THE REST STROKE.

TONE QUALITY

Anyone can play a *loud* note, but the object is to make a beautiful one. The movement that produces the best tone is quite subtle, although easy to perform when clearly understood. It is described in considerable detail because it is the single most important secret in the development of your individual touch, and is unfortunately ignored or inadequately described in most beginning books.

First consider the following analogy. Imagine that the string is a rope stretched in front of you a foot or so above the ground, and that you are going to make it vibrate by using a spade whose tip is curved in a half-moon shape (representing your nail).

The simplest way to make the rope vibrate would be to put the tip of the spade on the far side of the rope and pull it towards you. The rope would slide down to the extreme tip as you pulled, then would slip clear and be free to vibrate. This represents a note played with a head-on attack, which would produce good volume but a somewhat harsh tone.

For a more pleasing sound let us return to the rope and the spade. First, the handle of the spade would be angled to the left so that it was about 15 degrees away from the vertical (or at ten o'clock if that is easier to imagine). Next, the blade of the spade would be placed on the far side of the rope with the left cutting edge only in contact with it, at a point on the spade where the half-moon taper begins. The right edge would be just clear of the rope, so that the whole blade forms a slight angle away from it.

To produce the subtler vibration, you would draw the spade towards you angling it slightly to your right so that the rope would slide down the left hand cutting edge, be caught by the tip, and finally released. The amount of obstruction offered by the tip could be precisely controlled by the angle of the blade as the movement was performed; the flatter the blade to the rope, the more obstruction.

This essentially is the movement made by the nail when it plays a note, and the main secret of good guitar sound is contained in this basic movement.

Two final important points: First, the movement is made by the finger alone, and does not involve the whole hand. Second, the finger should have a comfortable curve, and this curve should be maintained throughout the stroke. Resist any tendency of the joints to straighten out when pull is applied to the string. In our analogy this would be the equivalent of using a spade with a rubber handle, which would be very hard to control with precision.

THE SHAPE OF THE NAILS

Before beginning your experiments, it is important to have the nail correctly shaped. Obviously if the nail is too long, it is liable to hang up on the string. If it is too short, it cannot give enough impetus to the stroke. Finally, if it is square in shape the corner will catch, making it almost impossible to play. If necessary, adjust the shape before proceeding.

File the nails so that a thin, even ridge may be seen above the fingertip when you look at your hand with the palm facing you. Finally, smooth the nails with fine (600 grade) sandpaper to remove any roughness left from the filing. This last step is essential if a scratchy tone is to be avoided when playing with the nails.

FINGER IDENTIFICATION

It is important to recognize how the fingers of each hand are identified, and this is shown in Fig. 7. The left hand is simple, the fingers being numbered 1-4 with no number for the thumb since it is not used. For the right hand the initial letters are used of the appropriate Spanish words: *P*ulgar=Thumb, *I*ndicio=Index finger, *M*edio=Middle finger and *A*nular=Ring finger.

Fig. 7 FINGER IDENTIFICATION.
These indications are universally used and should be memorized.

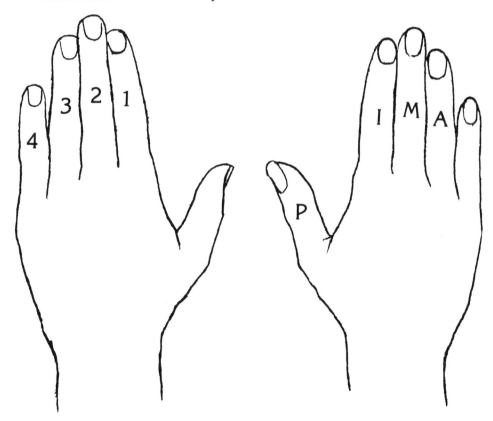

FIRST PRACTICE OF THE REST STROKE. ALTERNATION.

The movements described above should be tried out experimentally on the upper three strings. Try for a good quality note using first the index (*i*), then the middle (*m*) fingers. In playing a series of notes, always alternate the fingers. You may start with *i* or *m*—there is not fixed rule—but avoid using the same finger twice. Alternating the fingers produces a natural rhythm comparable to walking. Repeating the same finger is like hopping when you could walk. As one finger plays, the other should move forward to be ready to play in its turn.

THE LEFT HAND

The basic movements of the left hand are quite simple. The fingers press immediately behind the metal frets, shortening the vibrating length of the string and thereby changing its pitch.

The overall position of the left hand and wrist is of great importance. A good position ensures maximum reach, a minimum of excessive movement, and general stability. Of particular importance is the position of the thumb.

Fig. 8 LEFT-HAND POSITION.

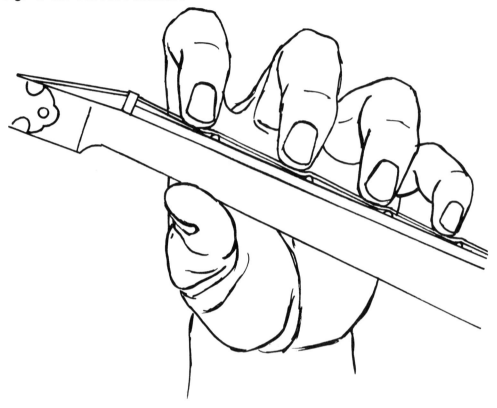

The illustration shows the correct position for the left hand with all fingers in place. The following points are important:

1. The thumb presses against the center of the back of the neck, just forward of the first fret. The pressure is as light as possible consistent with holding the strings down.

2. The first joint of the thumb does not bend. Allowing the joint to bend gives rise to insecurity in the left hand, since the thumb functions as a stable point of reference.

3. The fingers are as vertical as possible in relation to the fingerboard. Adjust the wrist to achieve this.

16

FIRST LEFT-HAND EXERCISE

The following exercise is excellent for stretching out and strengthening the left hand, and may profitably be practiced every day for the first few weeks.

1. With the thumb in the correct position, hammer down the first finger behind the first fret of the sixth string. Make as loud a sound as possible.

2. Leaving the first finger where it is, hammer in a similar way with the second finger behind the second fret.

3. Repeat the procedure with the third finger. Notice that it is much harder to reach right up to the third fret with the other two fingers in position; but try anyway, because this is an area where stretch must be developed.

4. Complete the movement by hammering with the little finger behind the fourth fret.

5. Repeat all the movements on the fifth and remaining strings. Remember to leave each finger down after it has hammered. On the third, second, and first strings it is harder to make the note sound with the left hand alone, but it *can* be done with practice.

PUTTING BOTH HANDS TOGETHER

The time has now arrived to co-ordinate the two hands in playing a series of notes. The right hand will play alternating rest strokes, and the left hand will move up a fret at a time as in the previous exercise.

1. Place the left hand first finger behind the first fret of the top (first) string. With the right hand play a firm rest stroke with the *i* finger.

2. Leaving the first finger in position, place the second finger behind the second fret. Play a rest stroke with the *m* finger.

3. Leaving the first two fingers down, continue to play the third and fourth frets, doing rest strokes with *i* and *m* in turn.

4. Repeat the procedure on the second and third strings.

FURTHER DEVELOPMENT

When you feel confident with the above exercise try it in reverse, playing from the fourth to the first fret on each of the top three strings. In working backwards it is not necessary to place all the fingers in advance. Simply start with the fourth finger, then the third and so on. As a final development try the following complete exercise.

1. Starting at the sixth string, play upwards from frets one to four, following on with the fifth and all other strings.

2. When you arrive at the highest point, the fourth fret of the first string, start down and play all strings from fourth to first fret. This is an excellent co-ordination exercise which will prepare your hands for playing from music.

THE FREE STROKE

For the sake of completeness we will consider briefly the other principal right hand movement known as the FREE STROKE.

The free stroke is easy to understand, since the movements are similar to those of the rest stroke except in the final phase. Instead of coming to rest, the finger just clears the adjacent string and comes to a halt in the air approximately above it.

Fig. 9 THE FREE STROKE.

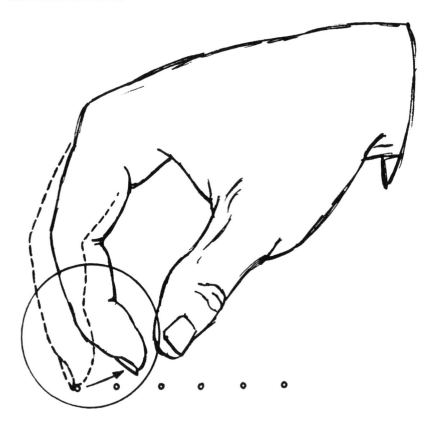

The free stroke becomes important in the performance of chords and arpeggios, which are considered in detail after sufficient notes have been learned. For now, the stroke may be practiced experimentally to distinguish it clearly from the rest stroke.

CONCLUSION

This first section on basic technique is a very important one, since at the end of it you are really playing the guitar. Remember particularly to check the following:

1. Is your sitting position correct, as in the illustration?
2. Is your left arm relaxed?
3. Is your thumb behind the neck? Not bent at the joint?
4. Are your left-hand fingers as vertical as possible when you play?
5. Are your right-hand knuckles on a line with the strings?
6. Is your right wrist correctly arched?

If the exercises have been thoroughly practiced and you can comfortably co-ordinate the two hands, you are now ready for the challenge and enjoyment of beginning to play from music.

NOTES ON THE FIRST STRING

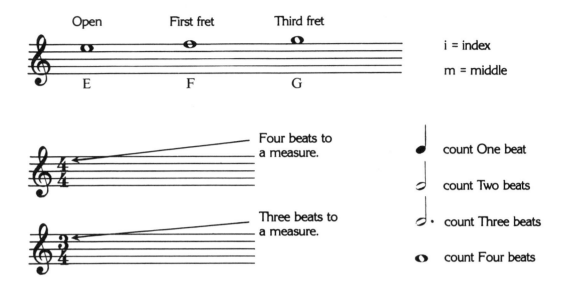

Open	First fret	Third fret
E	F	G

i = index

m = middle

Four beats to a measure.

Three beats to a measure.

♩ count One beat

𝅗𝅥 count Two beats

𝅗𝅥. count Three beats

𝅝 count Four beats

The diagrams above summarize the information necessary to play the exercises that follow. First memorize the three notes by playing them and saying aloud the letter names of the notes. Use rest strokes as learned in the previous section, and remember to alternate the fingers. With the left hand leave the fingers on where possible. For instance, when playing the progression F, G, F, the F should remain placed when you play the G. It is then ready when you want to play the F again.

COUNTING

Count the beats as you play, either out loud or in your head. It is the only sure way of measuring the time for each note, and if you form this habit at the very beginning you will progress much faster. Some people find that tapping the right foot helps to keep the beat even. The first beat of each measure should have a slight extra stress as it is the important downbeat (the conductor's baton always comes *down* on the first beat). Remember that you can go as slowly as you like as long as you give each note its proper time value.

Exercise 1

With this and all later exercises you are only concerned with the upper staff. The lower one is for the teacher.

The numbers beside the notes indicate left-hand fingering, *not the frets,* although they often coincide.

You will learn the notes more quickly if you do *not* write the letters (E, F, G, etc.) underneath them.

Exercise 2

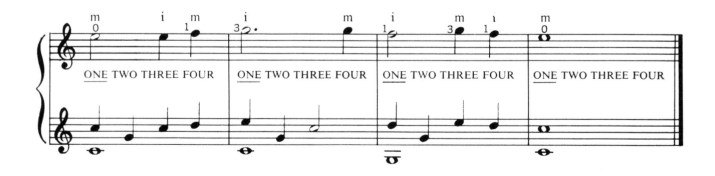

Exercise 3

Exercise 4

In this exercise the left-hand fingering has been omitted to ensure that you read from the notes rather than the numbers. Remember to keep up the alternation.

NOTES ON THE SECOND STRING

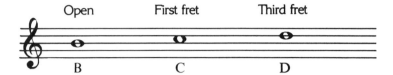

	Open	First fret	Third fret
	B	C	D

♩ = Quarter note rest

▬ = Half note rest

▬ = Whole note rest

RESTS AND DAMPING

Since a rest sign calls for a period of silence, it is necessary to be able to stop a string from sounding when a rest occurs.

With a stopped string (i.e. when a left-hand finger is used) all that is necessary is to release the pressure of the left hand finger from the fingerboard. The finger can still be in contact with the string; it is not necessary to take it off completely.

With an open string an easy way to damp the sound is to touch the string with the pad of the finger that would play next. For example, if you have just played the open first string with *i*, touch it with the pad of *m* to stop the sound. This may sound complicated, but is in fact very easy when you have done it a few times.

Exercise 5

In measure five, notice that the *i* finger is repeated. This is done sometimes after a long note or a rest, in cases when "changing step" results in smoother fingering in the measures to come.

In measure nine the fourth finger of the left hand is used on the G; this makes the transition from G to D smoother than a jump of the third finger.

23

Exercise 6

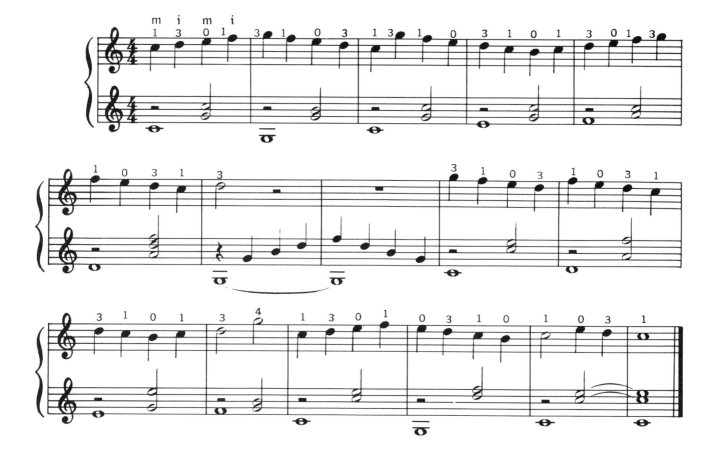

Exercise 7

As before, the left-hand fingering is omitted to check your note recognition.

PICK-UP NOTES

Music does not always begin on the first beat of the measure. There are sometimes one or more notes which precede the first stressed downbeat, and these are known as "pick-up" notes. When a piece begins with an incomplete measure, the final measure will also be incomplete, and the two will add up to one full measure.

The counting is not difficult as long as you identify which beat of the measure you start on, and count it accordingly. The song that follows shows how to do this.

THE BANKS OF THE OHIO   Traditional

NOTES ON THE THIRD STRING

Open   Second fret

G   A

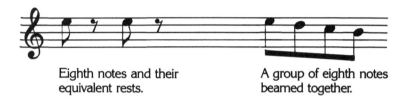

Eighth notes and their
equivalent rests.

A group of eighth notes
beamed together.

COUNTING EIGHTH NOTES

Eighth notes are twice as fast as quarter notes, so a way has to be found to divide the main counts in two. This is done by inserting the work "and" between the main counts.

Quarter Notes   ONE   TWO   THREE   FOUR

Eighth Notes   ONE and TWO and THREE and FOUR and

Notice that the number counts go at exactly the same speed in both examples, but the insertion of the "ands" in the second example gives the effect of doubling the time. Play and count the examples before going on to the exercises.

Exercise 8

Exercise 9

Exercise 10

This exercise is based on an extract from the song "Flow Gently Sweet Afton," music by James E. Spilman.

AURA LEE
George R. Poulton

NOTES ON THE FOURTH STRING

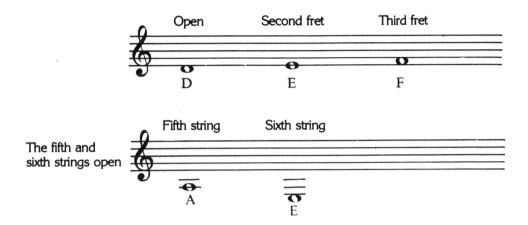

THUMB TECHNIQUE

The lower three strings are usually played with the thumb. The thumb may play a rest or a free stroke, the free stroke being by far the most common. The reason for this is that the lower strings tend to have greater natural resonance and therefore respond sufficiently to the lighter free stroke. In addition in a fast passage with the thumb; it is easier to repeat free strokes than rest strokes.

The thumb rest stroke does have its place, but this is usually reserved for passages of particular emphasis.

The illustrations demonstrate the two strokes, which should be tried experimentally before proceeding to the exercises.

Play Exercises 11 and 12, first with the free stroke, then for completeness try them with the rest stroke as well.

THUMB TECHNIQUE

Fig. 10 THE THUMB.

A. Like the fingernail the thumbnail is filed to an even curve.

C. Preparation. The string is in contact with the pad of the thumb, close to, but not touching the nail.

B. The angle of the thumb as it prepares to play.

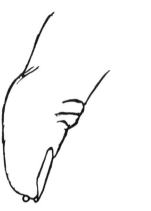

D. Completion, rest stroke. The thumb comes to rest against the next string.

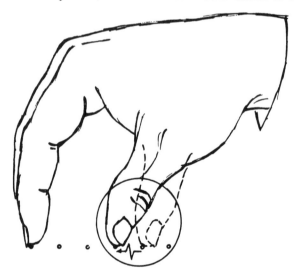

E. Completion, the free stroke. The thumb sweeps clear of the adjacent string.

F. This joint does not bend while doing either stroke.

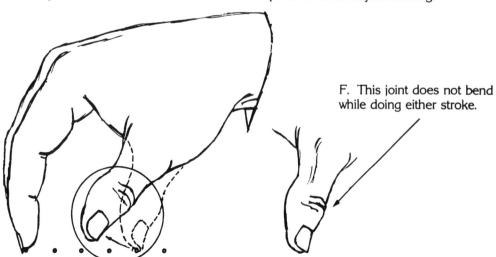

Exercise 11

Use the thumb throughout.

Exercise 12

Notice the use of the letter *p* to indicate the thumb, derived from the Spanish word "pulgar."

Exercise 13

This exercise is based on a famous chorale theme, for which J. S. Bach did many settings. In moving from thumb to fingers, try to avoid moving the hand. First use free strokes with the thumb, rest strokes with the fingers.

After you have played the piece a few times, try using free strokes with the fingers on all third-string notes, and rest strokes on the second and first strings. Although a little complicated to remember, this fingering will feel more natural.

NOTES ON THE FIFTH AND SIXTH STRINGS

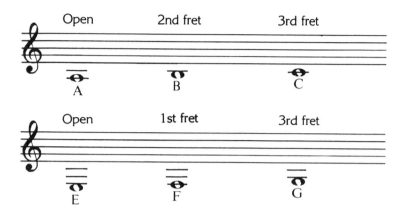

The notes below the staff are harder to memorize for some students, so the following exercises should be studied carefully and repeated where necessary. Distinguish particularly between the A on the *second* ledger line and the F on the *third*. In the same way be careful not to confuse the low E with the G since at first they look somewhat similar.

As soon as you are really familiar with these lower notes the way will be open to playing chords, arpeggios, and more complex pieces.

Exercise 14

In measure eleven notice that the fourth finger is used on the C, instead of the more usual third finger. This is to avoid jumping the third finger from string to string.

FANDANGO

Traditional

Exercise 15

The bass notes have been left unfingered so that you may check how well you know them.

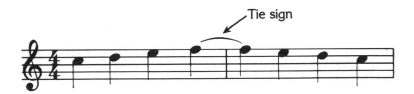

Tie sign

Ties

When two notes are joined by a TIE SIGN only the first is played, but it is held for the time value of both notes. This is particularly useful when a note is required to last from one measure to another.

In the example the F is held for two beats. The correct count for the two measures would be: "One Two Three *Four One* Two Three Four."

Exercise 16

SHARPS AND FLATS

Sharps (♯) and Flats (♭) are known as *accidentals* when they appear in the course of a piece. A sharp *raises* a note by a half step (one fret). A flat *lowers* a note by a half step.

Examples

A flat note a half step below an open string must be found on the next lower string. This will normally be at the fourth fret of the lower string.

Examples

The exception is the B flat, which is found at the *third* fret of the third string. You will remember from your tuning that the distance from the second to the third stirng is different from the others.

Example

A sharp or flat sign affects not only the note beside which it is placed, but all other occurrences of the same note for the remainder of the measure. Thus if an F is sharped at the beginning of a measure, all F's that follow in the same measure must also be sharped.

Example

both F's
are sharped.

This can be cancelled, however, by the use of a *Natural* sign (♮).

Example

both F's
are natural.

Play the example below several times until you fully understand the effects of the various accidentals.

Example

The F is natural because the ♯ sign
was in the previous measure.

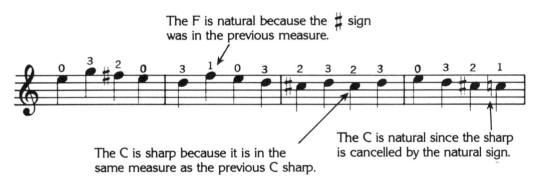

The C is sharp because it is in the
same measure as the previous C sharp.

The C is natural since the sharp
is cancelled by the natural sign.

Exercise 17

Exercise 18

MINUET

Henry Purcell

CHORD TECHNIQUE

Two or more notes played simultaneously are known as a chord. The technique used for chords is that of the free stroke for both fingers and thumb.

The illustration below shows a simple chord played by *i* and *m* on the top two strings. At the end of the movement both fingers are clear of the adjacent strings.

Fig. 11 A TWO-NOTE CHORD PLAYED BY *I* AND *M*.

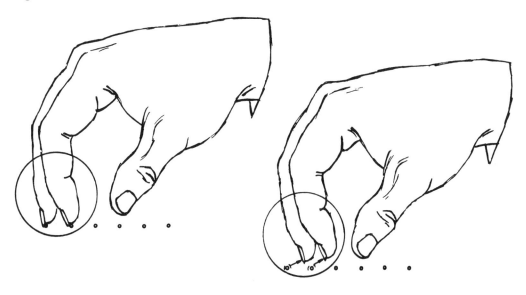

In Figure 12 the chord is played by the thumb and middle finger. At the completion of the movement, both thumb and fingers will be above the strings, but the *hand does not pull out from the strings*. The movement may be compared to an aircraft partially retracting its undercarriage without itself gaining height.

Whether there are two, three, or four notes in a chord, the technique is essentially the same. The important thing to remember is that the fingers should be placed in position on the strings before playing — do not snatch at the chord.

Fig. 12 A CHORD PLAYED BY *P* AND *M*.

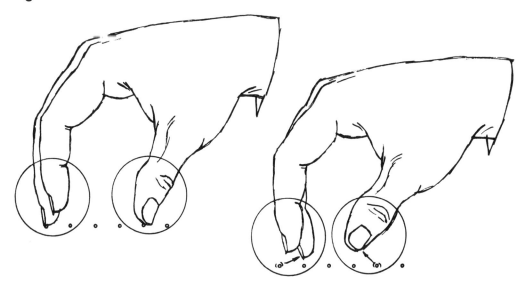

Exercise 19

This chord study introduces the use of the ring (*a*) finger, which becomes increasingly important as you progress with chords and arpeggios. Follow the right-hand fingering exactly, since it is comfortable and natural to the hand.

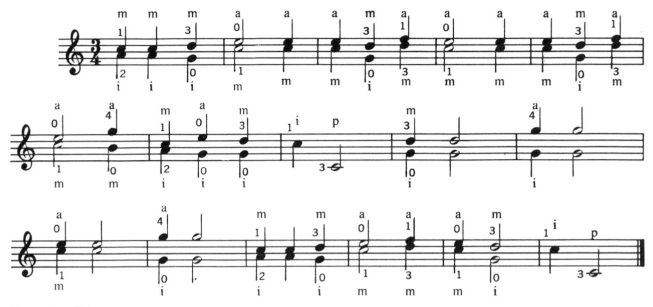

Exercise 20

Based on the popular Spanish theme "La Folia," this exercise starts simply but is progressive in difficulty. Remember not to lift the hand when playing the chords.

THE CHERRY SONG   Traditional

Exercise 21

All the chords may be played with *p, i* and *m*. Notice that although it may take longer to learn the notes at first the three note chords are not significantly more difficult to play.

ARPEGGIOS AND TRIPLETS

An ARPEGGIO is a broken chord, i.e. a chord whose notes are played in succession instead of simultaneously.

Example

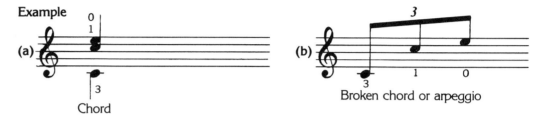

(a) Chord

(b) Broken chord or arpeggio

In example (b) the 3 above the group of notes shows that the three notes occupy the time of one quarter note. The group is known as a TRIPLET, and is counted "One - and - a" with three even syllables.

Example

Count: One and a Two and a Three and a Four and a

In a succession of triplets. as above, the three is often only indicated over the first group.

TECHNIQUE OF THE ARPEGGIO

The technique for playing arpeggios differs according to the direction of the notes played by the fingers. In the explanation below the two types of arpeggio are distinguished as "upward" or "downward" as shown in these examples.

Example

THE UPWARD ARPEGGIO
The direction of the notes played by
i and *m* is upward in pitch.

THE DOWNWARD ARPEGGIO
The pattern played by *m* and *i*
descends in pitch.

The Upward Arpeggio

This very common form of arpeggio starts with the selection of all the notes as if to play a chord. Then each finger plays a free stroke as shown in the illustrations.

Fig. 13 THE UPWARD ARPEGGIO.

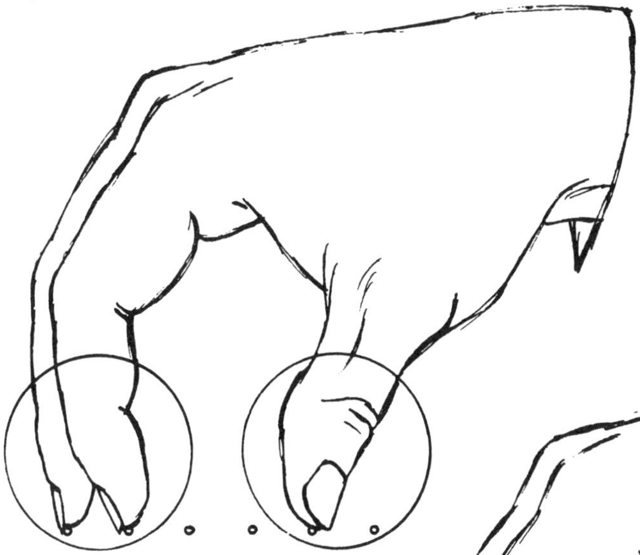

B. The thumb plays leaving the two fingers in position.

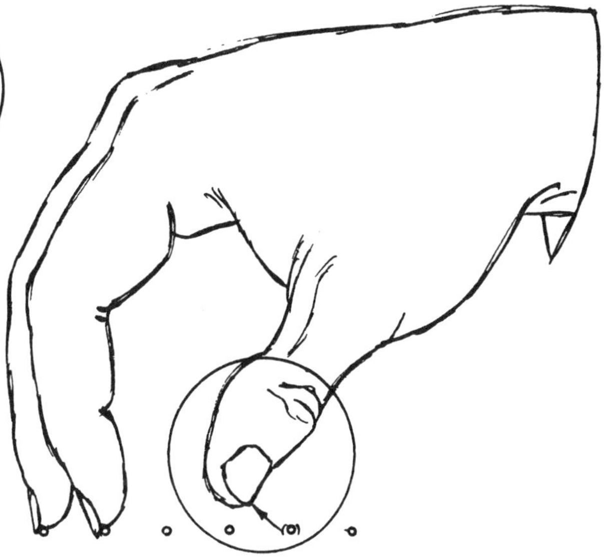

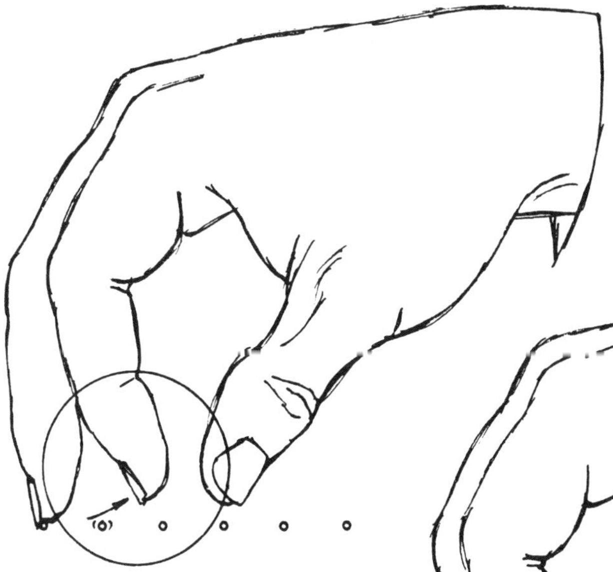

A. The fingers are prepared as if to play a chord.

D. The *m* finger plays completing the movement.

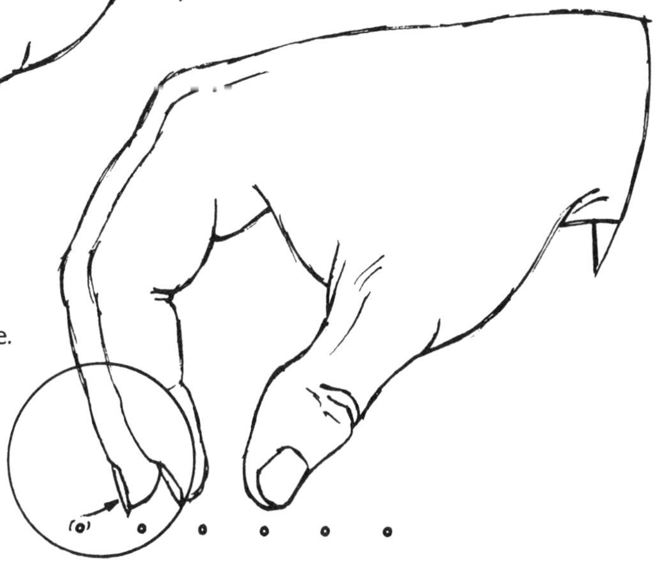

C. The *i* finger plays a free stroke.

The Downward Arpeggio

For the downward arpeggio *only the thumb and the finger on the highest string* are prepared in advance. Then the fingers play in succession as illustrated below.

Fig. 14 THE DOWNWARD ARPEGGIO.

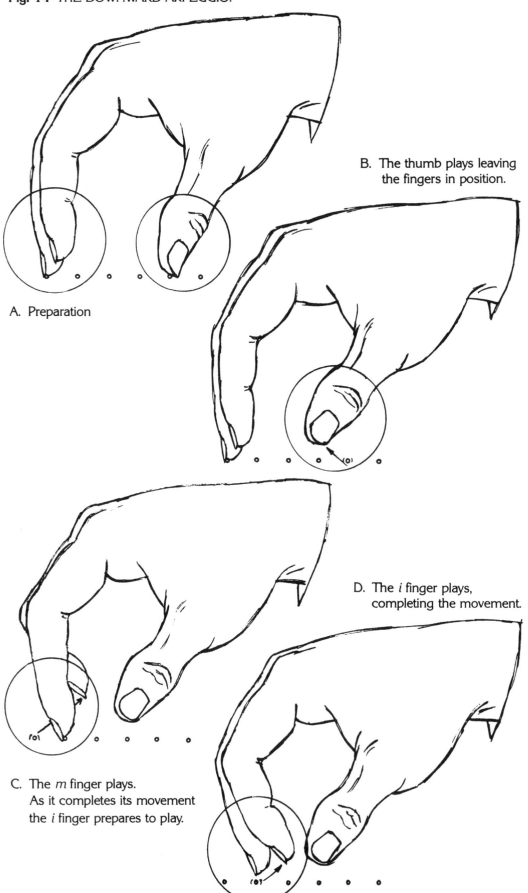

B. The thumb plays leaving
   the fingers in position.

A. Preparation

D. The *i* finger plays,
   completing the movement.

C. The *m* finger plays.
   As it completes its movement
   the *i* finger prepares to play.

Exercise 22

Play the chords first to learn the left-hand pattern, then practice the upward arpeggio.

Exercise 23

In this exercise the *m* finger should be in position before the thumb plays in each triplet group.

Exercise 24

Based on the study in three-note chords, this exercise may be used to practice the downward arpeggio as well.

COMBINING CHORDS AND MELODY

The main techniques for melody, chord, and arpeggio have now been learned; and the next step involves combining these techniques so that you will be able to play more interesting solos.

Melody and chords may be simply combined by holding one note of a chord while the other note is varied to form a melody.

Example

In (b) above the third finger remains on the low C so that it will continue to sound while the upper C, D and E are played.

Exercise 25

In this exercise the right-hand fingering shows that when chords and melody are mixed the alternation is not strict and fingers are occasionally repeated. Try to see from the music why this is done.

Use free strokes throughout.

Exercise 26

Use free strokes throughout

Sometimes the upper part of the chord is held while the lower part moves. The parts are often referred to as VOICES, since each may be compared to an individual singer.

In the example it would be usual to say that the movement is in the lower, or bass, voice.

The two voices do not necessarily start on the same beat, and often move quite independently.

Example

As complicated as this may look at first, it can be quite easily "solved" by considering what happens on each beat. Here is the procedure for playing the first measure:

First Beat   Play the low C to start the lower voice.

Second Beat   Play the high C to start the upper voice. The low C must continue sounding.

Third Beat   Play the upper voice E. The third finger is *still* on the low C so that it continues to sound.

The second measure proceeds as follows:

First Beat   Play the upper voice D

Second Beat   Play the open-string G. The fourth finger *remains on the high D* so that it continues to sound.

Third Beat   Play the F on the fourth string. The little finger is *still* holding down the D.

Work through the above steps until the procedure is quite clear. You will notice that there is no particular difficulty in reading music in two lines: The secret is to decide what happens on each beat.

LA VOLTA

16th-Century Dance

The repeat sign ‖: indicates that the first eight measures are played twice.

PRACTICE SUGGESTIONS

The pieces that follow have been chosen to enable you to practice all that you have learned so far, and to provide a beginning repertory of enjoyable music. They should be thoroughly studied before moving on to Part Two, and to ensure the best results the following suggestions are offered for practicing.

1. At this stage several short practice periods during the day will produce much better results than a single longer period.

2. Always take a break after about fifteen minutes of intensive practice. Your ability to learn is far greater after a pause for relaxation.

3. Do not attempt to practice when you are tired or not in the mood. You may feel virtuous, but the time is wasted.

4. Be patient with yourself and go slowly. This way the speed will come naturally in due course, and you will avoid the frustration that comes from trying to run before you can walk.

5. Keep in mind that the purpose is to make beautiful sounds, and that this can be done at an early stage and with very simple music.

6. At some time you will feel that your progress has been halted, and that you are on a plateau. This feeling is shared by almost everyone, and if you realize this and continue your regular practicing without feeling incompetent or discouraged you will soon pass through the stage and on to further achievement.

7. Realize that the difficulties you encounter are shared by most students. As

one example, the chord  which looks so simple on paper is very

difficult for almost all beginners. However, with practice the awkwardness disappears, and in time you will forget that it was ever a problem.

8. Enjoy yourself. Whatever your long-term goal may be the day to day practice can, and should, be a source of pleasure and satisfaction.

MOORISH DANCE

Traditional

EVENING BREEZE

F.M. Noad

ETUDE

Ferdinando Carulli (1770-1841)

In this piece the indication "Da Capo" means repeat from the beginning, "al fine" means "to the place marked *fine* or end." When playing Da Capo the other repeats are ignored.

MINUET THEME.

Wolfgang Amadeus Mozart (1756-1791)

FLAMENCO STUDY

Traditional

SONG AT NIGHTFALL

C.M. Bellman

Part Two

CONTENTS

TO THE READER

If you have successfully completed Part One of this course, you should now be used to the classical playing position, and to the principal right-hand techniques for the rest stroke, free stroke, chord and arpeggio. It should now be possible for you to count and play simultaneously simple tunes in the first position (i.e. using the first four frets), although you may have to go slowly to do this with accuracy. You should be familiar with note values from the whole note to the eighth note, the use of rests and ties, and the function of sharps and flats used as accidentals. Finally, you should be beginning to count and play at sight music in more than one part.

In this book you will extend both your practical and theoretical knowledge to include new notes on the fingerboard, new time values, the technique of the slur, and performance in a number of keys. The subject of keys is dealt with first, since progress in this area adds considerably to the variety of music that can be played.

As with the first book, a step-by-step approach will achieve the fastest results. Occasionally, you will feel that your forward progress has stopped and that you are on a plateau. The feeling is well known, and it is perhaps comforting to know that it is shared by almost everyone at some time. The quickest solution is to ignore the problem by keeping up regular practice and refusing to be discouraged. Then suddenly one day you realize that you are progressing after all.

This is not a difficult book, and I believe that there is much enjoyment to be had with the music in it; so welcome to this second stage and may your journey through it be entertaining and rewarding!

A NOTE TO THE TEACHER

This book continues the step-by-step learning of music and technique started by Part One, with a similar musical offering from different periods and styles. As before, I have included many duets, as I believe these to be enjoyable for both teacher and student, and thus to provide a strong incentive for continued study.

There are no bars or half bars in this book, because I agree with Besardus' instruction in the famous "Variety of Lute Lessons," of 1610, that recommends avoiding bars until "the hand be a little brought in use." However, the slur is introduced and covered in detail, as are the dotted quarter note and the notes of the second position. Faster notes and different time signatures advance the reading skills, and the all-important topic of where to use the rest stroke is approached. There is more emphasis on the use of the ring finger, and general principles of right-hand fingering are discussed.

The music is in general tuneful and varied and will, I hope, provide a pleasing addition to the basic repertoire offered in Part One.

KEYS AND SCALES

When a piece is said to be in a certain KEY, such as the "key of C major" or the "key of A minor," the indication is that a selected set of notes is used in the piece. That set of notes, when arranged in order, is known as a SCALE; thus the SCALE of C major contains the notes of the KEY of C major.

SCALE OF C MAJOR

The example shows one octave (eight notes) of the scale of C major. What distinguishes it from a random series of notes is the distance from one note to the next, in this case a WHOLE TONE or a HALF TONE.

On the guitar, these intervals are easy to understand, since from one fret to the next is a half-tone step; and from one fret to the one after next is a whole-tone step.

From E to F is a distance of one fret. Therefore, the step is a HALF TONE. From F to G is a distance of two frets, so the step is a WHOLE TONE.

To see if you understand this, try writing on the C major scale above the distance between each of the notes. Write either a one or a half between the notes to show whether the step is a whole or a half tone.

Always measure the distance between two notes on the same string. For instance, to measure from the first C to D, you must find the D on the same string as the C (i.e. at the fifth fret) to decide whether the notes are one or two frets apart.

If you have marked your scale correctly, you will have come out with the following arrangement:

1. Four notes with the distances between them WHOLE, WHOLE, HALF.

2. A WHOLE-TONE distance.

3. Another four notes with the distances between them again WHOLE, WHOLE, HALF.

The four-note groups are sometimes given the technical name of TETRACHORD, and the scale can be seen to be made up of two TETRACHORDS with the same arrangement of intervals, separated by a whole tone.

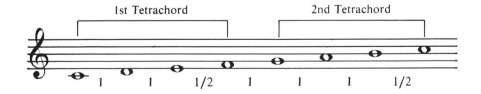

OTHER MAJOR KEYS

The purpose of explaining the arrangement of half and whole tones is to help you understand the following:

1. There is a logical arrangement to scales.
2. In terms of this arrangement of intervals, ALL MAJOR SCALES ARE THE SAME.
3. Any other major scale may be formed by starting on another note and keeping the same interval arrangement.
4. The other major scale will be named by the note on which it starts. The major scale formed by starting on the note G will be called the SCALE OF G MAJOR, and will contain the notes commonly used in the KEY OF G MAJOR.

Scale of G Major

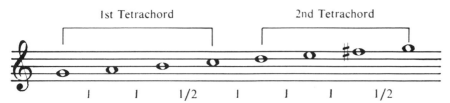

In the above scale of G major, notice that the construction is the same as that of the C scale, in that there are two groups of four (tetrachords), and each follows the arrangement of two whole steps and one half step. However, to make the upper four notes follow this pattern, it has been necessary to raise the F to F sharp.

As the F is always sharp in the key of G, a sharp is placed on the line representing F, after the clef sign, and becomes the KEY SIGNATURE or sign for G major.

This means that *all* F's must be played sharp, not just the one on the top line.

MINOR KEYS

The subject of minor keys and scales is dealt with at a later point. For the time being, it is sufficient to know that a given key signature may be for a major or *a related minor key*. To help you train your ear to distinguish minor from major, all succeeding pieces in minor keys are marked as such at the beginning. You will soon begin to recognize the characteristically melancholy sound of minor chords and arpeggios in contrast to the brighter, more cheerful sound of the major equivalents.

Exercise 1
THEME

J. S. Bach (1685-1750)

STUDY IN G MAJOR

Ferdinando Carulli (1770-1841)

(a) Note the change of finger to the fourth, which is necessary because the third finger is needed for the C that begins the next measure.

(b) Hold the low C until the next one is played. The dotted quarter note is fully explained on page 16.

COUNTING SIXTEENTH NOTES

Sixteenth notes are exactly twice as fast as eighth notes. When counting in quarter notes (3/4, 4/4, etc.), there will be four sixteenths to each number count, so two extra syllables or sounds are needed in addition to the One and Two and etc., used for counting eighth notes. The most widely used system adds an "e" sound after the number, and an "a" sound after the and, thereby producing the necessary four sounds to go with each number count.

Keeping the numbers absolutely even, try saying the following:

ONE	TWO	THREE	FOUR-e-and-a.
ONE	TWO	THREE-e-and-a	FOUR
ONE	TWO-e-and-a	THREE	FOUR
ONE-e-and-a	TWO	THREE	FOUR

Now try the same thing, tapping with your hand on a table, one tap to each syllable.

Finally, try doing the above while keeping a steady four beats with your foot. If you can do this and fit the four quick taps in at the right moment, you will have few problems with sixteenth notes.

The next step is to co-ordinate the count with notes on the guitar. For simplicity, use the open E at first, alternating the *i* and *m* fingers. Play the quarter notes slowly enough to allow time for playing the sixteenths without difficulty.

Notice that when playing these examples the fingers must work a little harder to produce even sixteenth notes. Thus, as well as a counting exercise, the above examples may also be used for technique practice to develop faster alternation.

Exercise 2

AIR ON A GROUND

Mixed Eighths and Sixteenths

Sixteenth notes are often grouped with eighths, as in the examples below. The counting principle remains the same, except that the extra syllable, shown below in brackets, may be omitted when the rhythm becomes familiar.

One (e) and   a   Two (e) and   a   One   e   and(a) Two   e   and(a)

Exercise 3 (Peruvian Dance)

ETUDE IN A MINOR (Op. 50, No. 13)

Mauro Giuliani (1781-1828)

The fingering in the second half of the fourth measure will seem awkward at first, but it is necessary to ensure a smooth change from the previous chord position. Remember that arpeggios are broken chords, so the left hand must try to select complete chords rather than individual notes one by one.

RIGHT-HAND FINGERING

Guitar music seldom has much fingering for the right hand (*p i m a,* etc.), and the few indications are usually intended to help you through some particularly difficult situations. Most of the time, therefore, it is necessary for the student to work out his own right-hand fingering, with corrections from his teacher, if he has one.

For this reason, it is necessary to look at some of the principles involved, so as to form good habits in the use of the right hand.

GENERAL PRINCIPLES

Single-Line Passages

A series of notes in a single line, such as a scale, is normally played by the alternation of *m* and *i*. Which of the two fingers is used first will depend on the particular situation, especially when string crossings are involved (see below).

Repetition of the same finger is permissible:

1. After a note of long value.

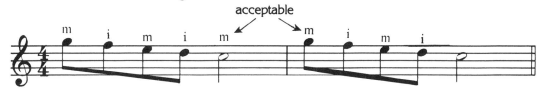

In a planned fingering, the half note gives a "breathing space" and enables the *m* finger to be used twice without awkwardness.

2. After a rest sign.

A Warning

Pulling the same finger across from one string to another is totally unacceptable, and is a bad habit formed by many beginners. Particular care should be taken to avoid this fingering, which invariably results in uneven scales and melodies.

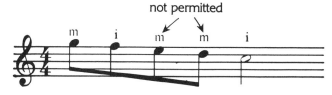

Two-Note Chords

In a succession of two note chords, the upper note may be played with alternating fingers:

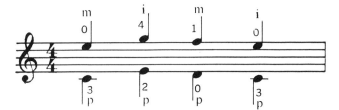

Some teachers prefer this fingering, on the basis that there is less tendency to pull the hand away from the strings. However, the simpler *p* and *m* fingering can also be used, providing that good chord technique is observed.

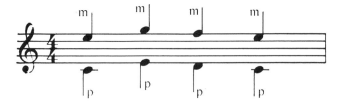

Exercise 4 (The Bishop's March — F.N.)

Practice first alternating *m* and *i* as shown in the first two measures. Then play the exercise again using *p* and *m*, taking particular care not to lift the hand when playing the chords. The combination *p* and *i* is sometimes more comfortable when the two notes are on adjacent strings, as in measure 9. Notice also that the thumb is used on the third string to avoid breaking up the regular pattern of fingering.

Crossing From String to String

In the above example, the crossing from the first to the second string is fingered with *m* on the open E, followed by *i* on the D. This is the normal string crossing used whenever practical. Similarly moving in the other direction, *i* normally plays the second string followed by *m* on the first string, e. g.:

However, sometimes situations arise which are not so easy to finger. For instance:

In playing the above, you will notice that keeping the alternation of *i* and *m* produces an awkward *m* to *i* crossing for the second D to E.

There are two acceptable solutions to this situation. The first is simply to practice the harder string crossing (*m* to *i*) until it becomes virtually as easy as the more normal *i* to *m*. This has the advantage of keeping strict simple alternation of *m* and *i*, but the less natural string crossing becomes a danger spot unless carefully planned out and practiced.

The alternative solution involves the use of the *a* finger in such a way that the more difficult string crossings are avoided.

Use of the Ring Finger ("a")

Using the same example, here is a fingering for the right hand that keeps the string crossings easy by using the *a* finger:

The string crossing *i* to *a* will be found to be comfortable, and the use of the *a* finger enables the second string crossing to be the simple *i* to *m* progression.

In general, the *a* finger tends to be weaker and less controllable, and for this reason most guitarists do exercises to develop and facilitate its use. Some exercises of this type will be found below which will feel quite awkward at first; but a dramatic change will be felt after a week or two of practice.

Exercise 5

Practice the upper fingering first, keeping strict time with the triplets. Then try the fingering below the staff. Use rest strokes throughout.

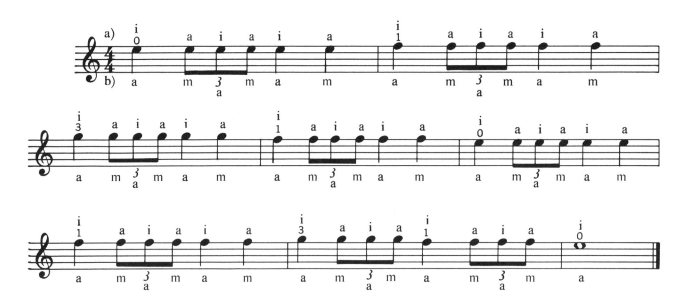

Exercise 6

In the third measure, the sign ③ shows that the B is to be played on the third string.

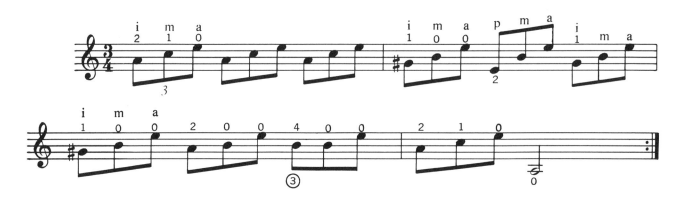

Exercise 7

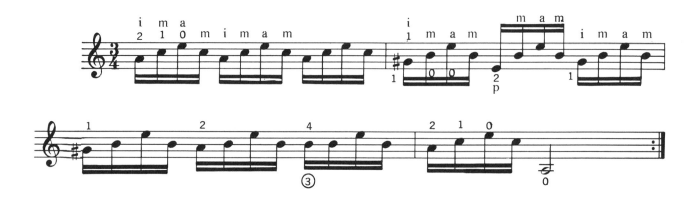

Exercise 8

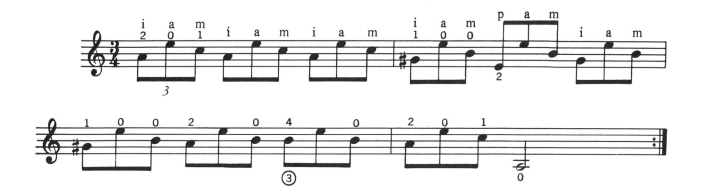

Exercise 9

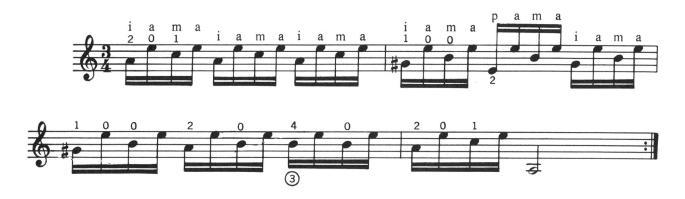

Exercise 10

This exercise is for the practice of string crossing, while keeping strict alternation of the index and middle fingers. Play slowly at first until the fingering is secure, then work to increase the speed.

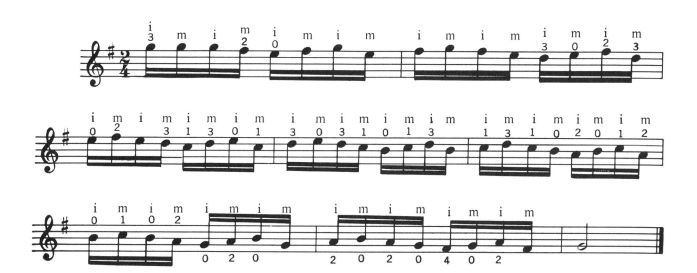

THE DOTTED QUARTER NOTE

A dot added to a note increases its value by half. Thus the half note, which normally lasts for two beats, is increased to three beats when dotted.

Similarly, a quarter note when dotted is increased from one to one and a half beats, and is equivalent in duration to a quarter note tied to an eighth note.

The counting of the dotted quarter note must be clearly understood and practiced at this point, to avoid future difficulties.

First, count and play the following simple combination of quarters and eighths:

Now, with the first quarter tied to the following eighth, count the measure in exactly the same way, but hold the initial note through the count of ONE and TWO:

Now count the dotted quarter in exactly the same way:

The all-important point to remember is that in all times counted in quarter notes (i.e. 3/4, 4/4, etc.) the dotted quarter has *two number counts* wherever it occurs in a measure. This should be clear when you have worked through the examples below.

Count and play each of the following:

The two familiar tunes that follow demonstrate the characteristic "skip" of the dotted quarter followed by an eighth.

Exercise 11 (Welsh Lullaby)

(a) This note, A, is at the 5th fret. To play it, slide the 3rd finger as indicated.

Exercise 12 (Greensleeves)

A minor

PACKINGTON'S POUND

Anon. (16th Century)

A minor

RIGHT-HAND TECHNIQUE

Choice of the Rest or Free Stroke

The basic techniqes for rest and free strokes are fully explained in Part I of this series, which should be consulted if there is any uncertainty about the execution of these basic and important movements. The time has now come to try to establish some general rules covering when to use each of these strokes; a difficult task since there is a lack of agreement between even the best performers on this subject. The choice of stroke is probably best considered in relation to specific situations of chords, scale passages, and arpeggios, and to passages which mix these elements together.

Single-Note Passages

When playing duets, you will already have noticed that the rest stroke gives the best quality and fullest sound to the melody part when a single line is involved. It might thus seem easy to make an absolute rule and say that all such melodies should be played with the rest stroke throughout. However, just as a diet of cake with never a slice of bread would eventually seem too rich, so the unrelieved rest stroke, as beautiful as it is, can suffer for want of variety.

Nevertheless, single-note melodic or scale passages are customarily played with extensive use of the rest stroke, and when speed is involved most players find the rest stroke the most accurate and reliable.

Chords

As a general rule, chords are played with the free stroke by both thumb and fingers. The exceptions to the rule may be considered in relation first to two-note chords, then those involving more notes.

Two-Note Chords

Chords of only two notes, both of which are played by the fingers, are invariably played free stroke. In cases where the bass note is played by the thumb and the melody note by a finger, the rest stroke is sometimes used by the finger to bring out or accent the melody.

All Melody Notes—Rest Stroke

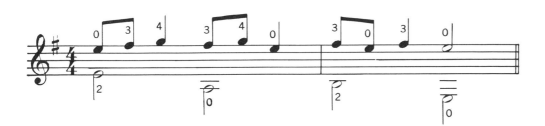

In the example, all the upper part *may* be played with the rest stroke. However, the rule does not say that it must be used, but simply that the option is there for increased volume or fullness of sound, when required for the best musical effect. In the above case, the thumb would use the free stroke—for both to use the rest stroke would be impossibly cumbersome.

Fig. 1 PREPARATION: TWO-NOTE CHORD WITH REST STROKE
The thumb and index finger prepare the chord in the usual way.

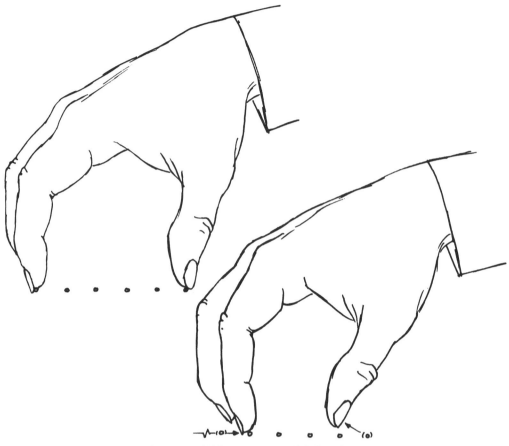

Fig. 2 COMPLETION: TWO-NOTE CHORD WITH REST STROKE
The index finger comes to rest on the second string as the thumb moves clear of the fifth string. The rest of the hand should not move.

Play the example first with free strokes, then with rest strokes for the melody, and compare the different effects produced.

Often, just an occasional rest stroke is used to bring out particular notes. In the example below, the rest strokes are indicated by the sign ▽.

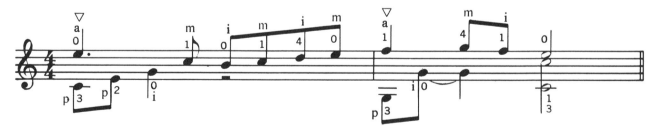

Play the above both with and without rest strokes, so that your ear can clearly distinguish the effect produced.

When playing two-note chords with a rest stroke on the upper note, it is permissible to arpeggiate the notes very slightly, i.e. to play the thumb fractionally before the finger. The separation should be very small, so that the sound is almost simultaneous. This arpeggiation makes the rest stroke easier to play at first, but care must be taken not to lose the beat when using this device.

Exercise 13

Use rest strokes throughout for the melody.

Exercise 14 (The Piper's Tune)

Use rest strokes where marked with the sign ▽.

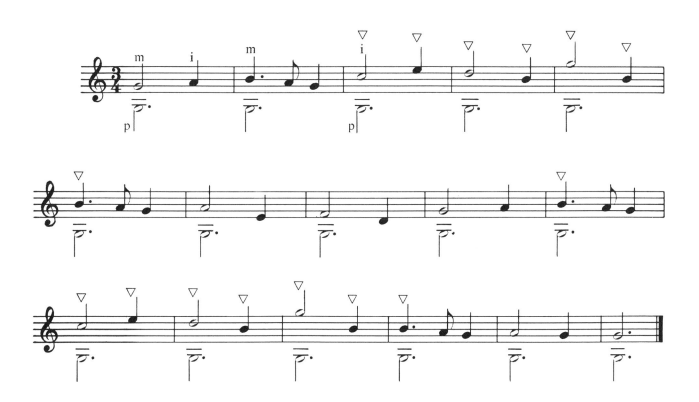

Chords of Three or More Notes

In chords which involve more than just two notes, the fingers *always use the free stroke.* On very rare occasions, the thumb may use rest strokes for particular emphasis. However, this is not considered worth illustrating, since the bass strings are by their nature so strong that the additional emphasis of the rest stroke is almost never needed and does not warrant special practice at this time.

Arpeggios

As you have already learned, the basic technique of the arpeggio involves the use of the free stroke. However, unless the arpeggio is simply an accompaniment to a song or another instrument, it will be found that there is frequently a "secret" melody contained in some of the notes of the arpeggio. Actually, we wish this melody to be anything but secret, and here again the rest stroke proves its value as a means of emphasizing and bringing out certain notes.

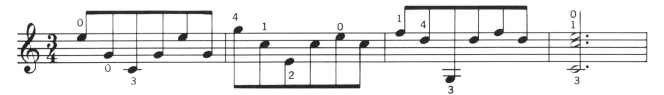

The example above contains both a melody and an accompaniment. The first step is to play it and to see if you can identify the concealed melody.

Now play the tune below, and see if this agrees with what you heard when playing the arpeggio.

Of course, the two elements would have been easier to identify if the passage had been written like this:

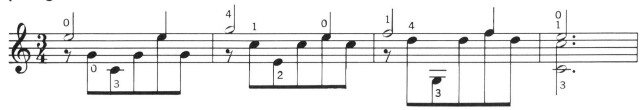

You will notice that the notes intended as melody all have an upward stem which makes them easy to identify. However, music is not always written this way, and sometimes it will be up to you to discover and bring out the hidden melodies.

Returning to the first example, try the passage now with rest strokes where you see the sign ▽.

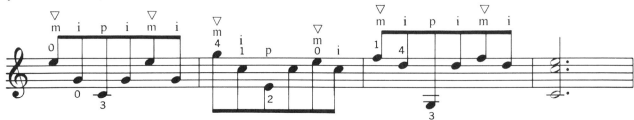

It takes a little practice to become used to mixing rest strokes in with arpeggios, but the work is amply rewarded by the resulting musical effect.

General

The rest stroke may be considered in many ways to be the technique that produces the best and fullest tone quality. A player who uses this technique freely will have a stronger touch and greater variety in his playing than one who confines himself to the free stroke. Of course, the free stroke can be developed with practice to sound very similar to the rest stroke, but there is still a lack of contrast and fullness in the unrelieved use of the free stroke.

The exercises and studies that follow give specific indications of where to use the rest stroke. Try to see the reasoning involved, and in later pieces to apply the same principles whether or not the rest strokes are specified. In this way, you will be on your way to acquiring the professional sound associated with skilled use of the rest stroke.

LESSON IN C MAJOR

Napoleon Coste (1806-1888)

STUDY IN C MAJOR

Fernando Sor (1778-1839)

VICTORIAN SONG

Frederick Noad

The letters D. C. at the end of the piece are an abbreviation for Da Capo,
meaning "Repeat from the beginning." Al Fine means "Up to the place
marked Fine [the end]."

SOLITUDE

Frederick Noad

A minor

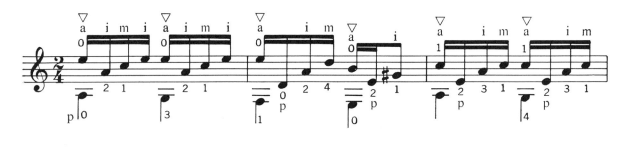

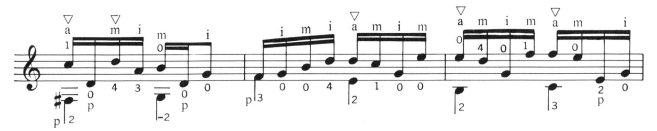

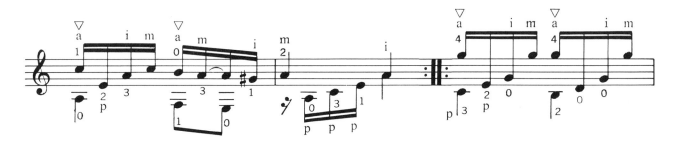

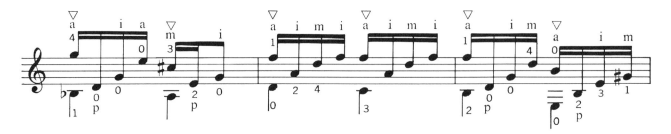

THE SLUR OR LIGADO

It is sometimes desirable to join two or more notes together in a way that is smoother than the usual way of playing. When notes are linked in this way, they are said to be SLURRED. Special techniques are used to accomplish this, differing according to the upward or downward direction of the notes to be slurred. The Spanish word LIGADO is also used, and literally means "bound together."

TECHNIQUE OF THE UPWARD SLUR

Upward Slur

Upward Slur

The example above shows an open B linked to a C with the conventional sign for a slur. To execute this, play the open B in the usual way, then sound the C with the left hand only by hammering the first finger down firmly behind the first fret. This technique is popularly known as the HAMMER-ON because of the action of the left-hand finger.

In the above example, the two notes to be linked are both fretted, i.e. neither is an open string. In this case, both notes must be prepared in advance; the first finger in position on the C at the first fret, and the third finger above the D ready to hammer down. As before, the right hand plays the C in the usual way, while the second note, the D, is played by the action of the left hand alone.

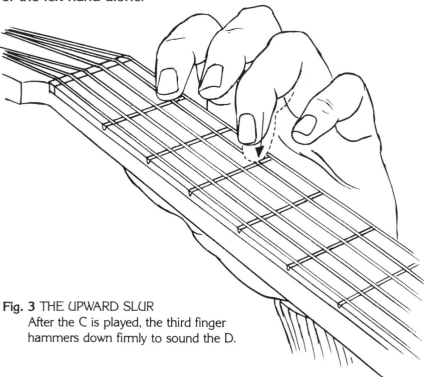

Fig. 3 THE UPWARD SLUR
　　After the C is played, the third finger
　　hammers down firmly to sound the D.

These are the points to remember:

1. When the first note is played, the finger that is to hammer should be in position about a quarter inch above the point where it will strike.

2. In spite of the short distance it travels, the hammer stroke must be decisive enough to make a clear note.

3. It is important to hammer immediately behind the fret. This produces the clearest note.

In general, the upward slur is not difficult to perform, and in many cases will make a passage easier to play.

Now here are some exercises covering the most usual types of upward slur in approximate order of difficulty. Aim to play each pattern with evenness and clarity before moving on to the next. Do not be alarmed by the number of sharps and flats necessary to illustrate the patterns. In fact, the left-hand fingering corresponds in each case to the fret number, so if the fingering shows first finger going to second, then the slur is from the first to the second fret. This coincidence makes it almost possible to read the exercises from the fingering alone.

Exercise 15

Exercise 16

Exercise 17

Exercise 18

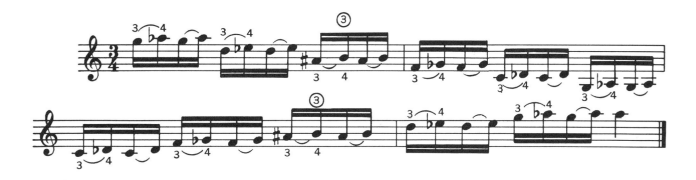

Exercise 19

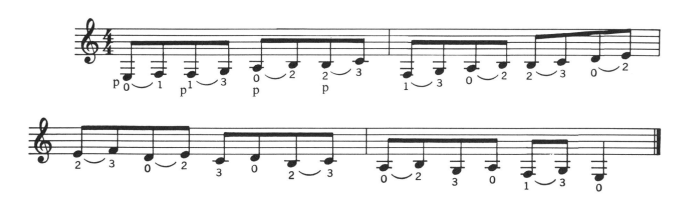

Exercise 20 (The High Trail — F.N.)

WALTZ (Op. 10, No. 6)

M. Carcassi (1792-1853)

THE DOWNWARD SLUR

When the slur direction is downward, a different method is used to play the second note, since a hammer stroke is not practical.

Slurring to an Open String

The simplest form of downward slur occurs when the second note is an open string.

To play the above example, sound the C in the usual way; then, with the left hand alone, play the second note by pulling sideways with the first finger to sound the open B. At the completion of the movement, the first finger should be touching the fingerboard and the side of the first string.

Do not try to clear the first string with the fingertip by pulling *upwards*. It is harder to make a clear sound this way, and it is only done in the rare circumstance that the adjacent string must continue to sound, i.e.

The general rule is to aim for a distinct, clear note by pulling across the string and coming to rest on the fingerboard.

The Downward Slur Between Two Frets

When neither string is open, both notes must be prepared before the first is played.

To play the above example, place *both the first and third fingers* before playing the D. After the right hand has played the D, the left-hand third finger pulls sideways to sound the C. As before, it comes to rest on the fingerboard and in contact with the E string.

A popular term for the descending ligado is the PULL-OFF. This expresses the movement quite well and serves as a reminder that it is necessary to pull the finger off rather than just take it off.

Fig. 4 THE DOWNWARD SLUR
    After the D is played, the third finger pulls the string in the direction shown to sound the C.

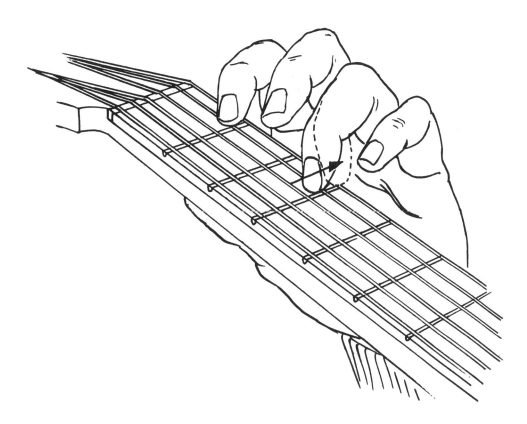

Exercise 21

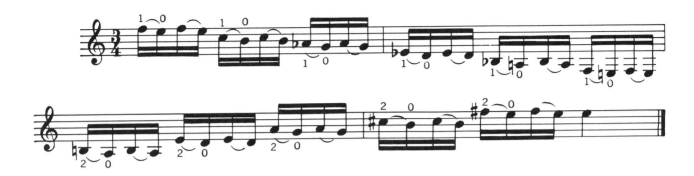

Exercise 22

Exercise 23

Exercise 24

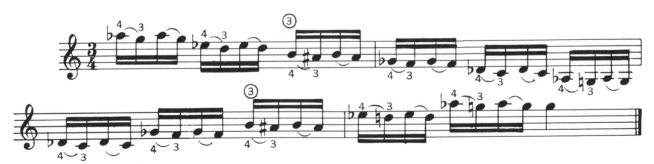

Exercise 25 (The Periwig — F.N.)

STUDY IN D MINOR

Frederick Noad

THE SECOND POSITION

The "positions" on the guitar are governed by the location of the left hand. When the hand is placed so as to reach frets 1-4, this is known as the *first position*. When the left hand is moved up the fingerboard so that it can reach frets 2-5, it is said to be in the *second position*. Thus the position can always be identified by the lowest fret within reach of the hand; this is also the fret normally played by the first finger.

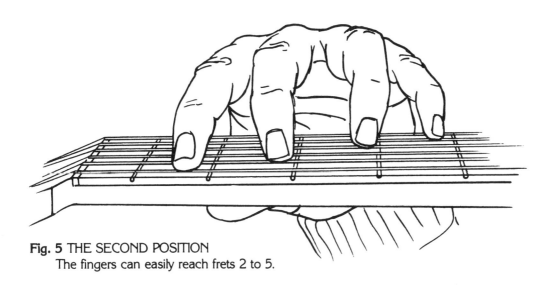

Fig. 5 THE SECOND POSITION
The fingers can easily reach frets 2 to 5.

Since the first four frets have already been learned, it is only necessary to add the notes at the 5th fret to complete the second position.

NOTES AT THE 5TH FRET

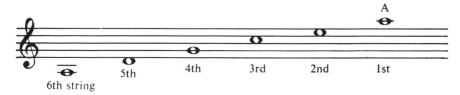

You will notice that, with the exception of the high A which is new, all the other notes are duplicates of notes already learned.

CHANGING POSITION

Very often, a change of position must be made because the indicated fingering requires it, e.g.

The fourth-finger indication on the A shows that a move to the second position is necessary. The point to remember is that the whole hand must move, not just the finger.

USE OF THE GUIDE FINGER

Sometimes the playing of two successive notes by the same finger becomes a smooth way of changing position.

In moving from the G sharp to the A, the fourth finger maintains contact with the string. As it goes up, the hand goes with it, making the change from first to second position.

KEY OF D MAJOR

Certain keys are particularly well suited to certain positions, because in these positions more of the required notes for that key lie under the hand. The second position is useful when playing in the key of D, which requires that both F's and C's be sharped.

SCALE OF D MAJOR

Notice that this single-octave scale, although fingered in the first position, may be played in either first or second position. However, when the scale is extended as far as possible in both directions, the second position becomes the most useful.

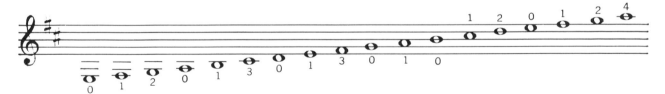

Play the above several times for familiarity with the position before trying the exercises below.

Exercise 26 (Theme by Purcell)

Exercise 27 (The Willow — F.N.)

STUDY IN D (Op. 44, No. 14)

Fernando Sor

COUNTING IN EIGHTH NOTES

3/8 AND 6/8 TIMES

So far, the only time signatures used have been 2/4, 3/4, or 4/4, indicating respectively two, three, or four quarter notes to the measure. However, the eighth note is often used as a counting unit, and the time signatures 3/8 and 6/8 are very common.

Three-Eight Time (3/8)

The example below shows basic counting rules applied to 3/8 time.

The points to remember are these:

1. Each eighth note receives a number count. The "ands" are used to help count the sixteenth notes.

2. Quarter notes now receive *two* counts.

3. The dotted quarter note receives three counts.

4. Dotted eighth notes are counted in exactly the same way as dotted quarter notes in 4/4 time.

It would be logical to suppose that pieces written with an eighth-note count would be faster (perhaps twice as fast) than those with a quarter-note count. Unfortunately, this is not so, and sometimes extremely slow pieces are written in 3/8 or 6/8. One of the reasons for this is that the shorter-value notes take up less space, so a slow piece that would take several pages if written out in long notes can be compressed onto a page or two, and for musicians the fewer page turns the better.

The speed of a piece is known as its TEMPO, and tempo is indicated by a word, usually Italian, at the very beginning above the first line. The commonest tempo markings are:

Largo	Very slow, broad
Lento	Slow
Adagio	Slow, literally, at ease
Andante	Walking speed
Moderato	Moderate
Allegretto	Fairly fast, but not as fast as Allegro
Allegro	Quick, literally, cheerful
Presto	Fast

Exercise 28 (Theme by de Viseé)

6th to D

ANDANTINO (Op. 35, No. 2)

Fernando Sor

Six-Eight Time (6/8)

The signature 6/8 is used to denote a time consisting of two triplets in each measure. There is, in addition to the usual accent on the first count, a second accent on the fourth count which begins the second triplet.

6/8 time can be considered in two ways; as six eighth notes or as two triplets. The sort of time which can be divided into triplets this way is known as "compound time." When learning a new piece, and when the tempo is slow, the count of six should be used, and this applies to the examples below. Later, when you are thoroughly familiar with a 6/8 piece and wish to play it at a fast tempo, you may find it more convenient to count just the two triplet beats.

Exercise 29 (Theme by Hook)

6th to D

119

ALLEGRETTO, (Op. 50, No. 12)

Mauro Giuliani

DYNAMIC MARKINGS

Loud and soft are usually indicated by abbreviations of the Italian; Forte (loud) and Piano (soft). A single *f* is used for loud, *ff* for extra loud, *fff* for about as loud as possible. In a similar way, softness is graded from *p* to *ppp*. The letter *m* (for Mezzo) means moderately. Thus *mf* means moderately loud.

A gradual increase in sound is usually indicated by two lines which gradually move apart.

These signs are placed below the staff. The reverse, a decrease in sound, is shown by the same sign reversed, i.e.

The Italian words used are *crescendo* for increasing in volume and *decrescendo* or *diminuendo* for the corresponding decrease. They will more often be seen in their abbreviated form of *cresc., decresc.* and *dim.*

CONCLUSION

The extra pieces below are offered for additional practice and enjoyment. Many students like to take the time to learn an extra piece or two before moving on to new topics. This serves to consolidate what has been learned, as well as continuing to strengthen the hands in preparation for harder techniques. It is also very important to take the time to enjoy music without working too hard, for instance, by playing earlier pieces which will now seem much easier than they did. This is also a good way to realize the progress that you have made, and perhaps to be surprised by it.

PAVANE

Anon. (16th Century)

A minor

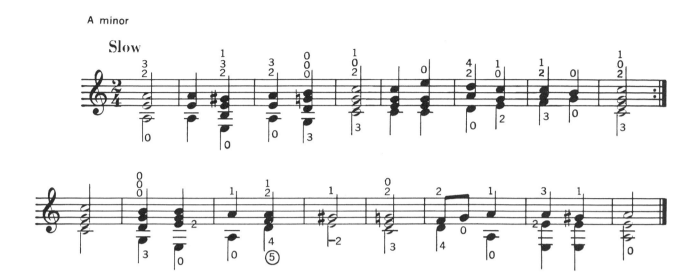

ZAPATEADO

Spanish Traditional (arranged by F. N.)

124

MINUET, (OP. 21, NO. 12)

M. Carcassi

EL VITO

Spanish Traditional (arranged by F. N.)

SONATINA

Thomas Attwood (1765-1838)

STUDY IN C (OP. 51, NO. 2)

Mauro Giuliani

Part Three

CONTENTS

TO THE READER

If you have completed Parts I and II of *First Book for the Guitar* I hope that you will have discovered that the reading of music is straightforward and logical, with few mysteries, provided that it is approached in reasonable stages.

In Part III you will explore some new keys, and find that, although there may be more sharps to remember, there are no additional technical difficulties that compare with using the black keys of the piano. You will learn some new counting techniques that will lead to more sophisticated rhythms, and you will learn the beginnings of barring with your left hand.

But there is no sudden leap in difficulty, and progress through this volume should be at about the same pace as in Parts I and II.

Suggestions for further progress will be found at the end of the book, as well as a self-test for you to check your skills. If you have reached this point without undue difficulty, you are undoubtedly on the way to great enjoyment of the guitar. Welcome to this next stage.

NOTE TO THE TEACHER

Part Three of *First Book for the Guitar* completes the trilogy of first-year study methods by covering the half bar, keys from F to E major and D to E minor, more complete rhythms including syncopation, and, in general, more emphasis on variety and expression in performance.

I have still avoided the full bar and, except for momentary excursions, the higher positions. This is in no way an attempt to avoid these areas or to encourage students to avoid them; it stems from the conviction that with a good basic knowlege of reading and technique the next stages of position playing will follow logically and without undue difficulty.

Some students will progress very rapidly through these books and may perhaps question the step-by-step approach. However, because in my experience such students are in the minority, the purpose here is to write for the interested many as well as the exceptional few.

Teachers will find a fairly logical transition to *Solo Guitar Playing,* Volumes I and II, which deal with the higher positions in stages and with a similar duet approach. There is some overlapping of the first part of *Solo Guitar Playing,* Volume I, but I believe many students will welcome some additional easy repertoire for recreation. My hope is that the basic knowledge acquired in these three preliminary stages will make the transition to the more advanced books both smooth and enjoyable.

A PRACTICAL WARM-UP ROUTINE

For those with limited practice time, it is often difficult to decide the best way to divide that time in order to achieve a maximum of improvement and enjoyment. For most people the two are interlinked; that is, some degree of progress is neccessary for a continued enjoyment of playing. So it becomes necessary to give some part of the available time to increasing dexterity, as well as to the exploration of new pieces, improvement of sight reading, etc.

There is a danger in becoming too caught-up with exercises. Some students develop a rather rigid approach and for days and weeks at a time confine themselves to exercises in the hope that such strictness will bring about a technical breakthrough. Usually there is some improvement in dexterity, but this is only noticeable in the exercises, since the musical pieces have been neglected and do not immediately reflect the new strengths.

One approach is to use a fixed series of exercises which is repeated daily as a prelude to playing. A sample routine is given below, which should work well and provide continued improvement if the following points are observed:

1. Start slowly, increasing speed gradually as the muscles warm up.
2. Do not stop until the routine has been completed; part of the value lies in the continuity.
3. Try for complete accuracy—careless playing will not achieve much.
4. Do the routine every day.

DAILY PRACTICE ROUTINE

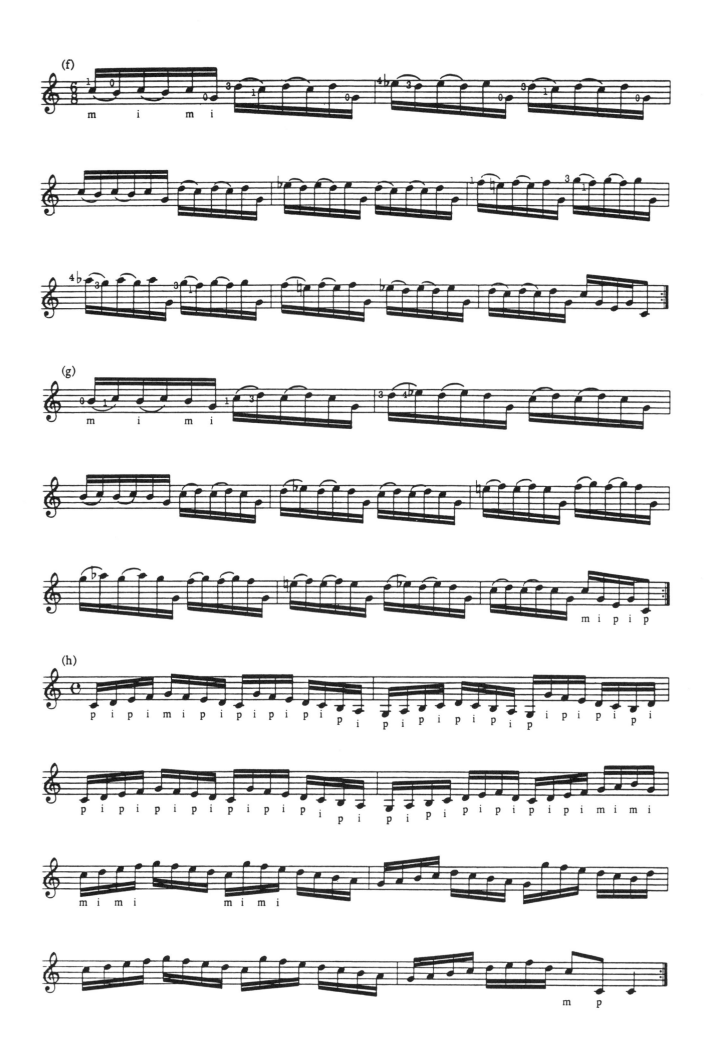

(i)

p i p i p i p i p i p i p m i p i m i m

i m i m

Notes on the Routine

a) For slow chord practice. Continue on volume and clarity, with each note distinctly audible. Play it at least twice, but several times, if necessary, for even results.

b) A simple arpeggio, to be played with full volume until a precise regularity is achieved.

c) A development of the previous arpeggio. This pattern gives extra practice to the less coordinated m. and a. fingers and is a valuable exercise.

d) Use this arpeggio to practice bringing out the first note of each group with a rest stroke.

e) A more challenging arpeggio, possibly the most useful pattern for developing coordination. This should be practiced until it is crystal clear and even-sounding.

f) An easily memorized exercise for the descending slur. Repeat as many times as is necessary for clarity, remembering to pull into the fingerboard rather than outward from the string.

g) The same exercise for the ascending slur.

h) To be practiced in two ways. First using the fingering shown, then with simple alternation of i and m. When using the latter fingering, use free stroke on the lower strings, rest stroke on the upper two. Both fingers will be found useful, the choice depending upon the particular context. In general the p. i. fingering has less tendency to displace the right hand; however, the m. i. fingering tends to sound more even.

i) This commonly encountered formula provides good practice for general coordination.

MORE ADVANCED COUNTING

The Dotted Eighth Note

In 3/8 and 6/8 time the dotted eighth note presented little problem, since it was counted in the same way as a dotted quarter note in 4/4 time. (Part II, page 44.) In 4/4 time, however, a different formula is needed, since the basic counting unit is the quarter note, not the eighth.

The dotted eighth note is customarily followed by a sixteenth, and together they make a complete quarter note beat.

The dotted eighth note may be considered as three sixteenths, since the dot has increased the eighth note (= 2/16) by half. Using the sixteenth note counting formula (Part II, page 6), we arrive at the following:

One - e - and - a   Two - e - and - a   Three - e - and - a   Four - e - and - a

When used with quarter or eighth notes, it is perhaps easiest at first to use the sixteenth-note count on all notes:

One - e - and - a   Two-e-and-a   Three - e -and - a   Four - e - and-a

However, when the time is understood, the count may be simplified as follows:

One (e-and) a   Two   Three - and   Four.

Now try counting each of the following examples, first the sixteenth-note method, then simplified as above. As you count, tap with your hand in time to the notes as written.

GRACE NOTES

Grace notes are a form of decorative embellishment popular with composers of all periods. Written as small notes, they have no time value of their own but borrow their value from the note to which they lead.

To execute the above, play the small note and instantly pull off to sound the second (main) note. Practice the above until the grace note can be played extremely fast but with clarity and snap.

Sometimes the direction from the grace note to main note is upwards, in which case the technique of the upward slur is used.

The instant that the grace note is sounded, the main note should be hammered on by the left hand.

A slur sign is sometimes (but not always) given between the grace and main notes. Whether indicated or not, always use slur technique with this type of grace note.

ANDANTE   Fernando Sor, Op. 35, No. 14

Syncopation

Syncopation is a term applied to rhythms that alter the usual pattern of accents. In 4/4 time, for instance, there is a conventional accent on the first beat of the bar, which is altered if we tie notes over in this sort of arrangement:

Very often the other part (in the example below, the bass) will follow the conventional accent pattern, which serves to make the syncopated line stand out, thus:

The beats can also be divided into eighth notes, as in this typical ragtime formula:

The duet below serves to illustrate typical syncopation with an extract from one of the most popular of all ragtime tunes.

Exercise 1

From "The Entertainer"   Scott Joplin

148

THE HALF BAR

The-left hand finger may be used to stop more than one string at the same time. The technique is known as "barring," since the finger is placed sideways across the strings like a bar. When five strings or less are covered, the rather imprecise expression "half bar" is used.

Learning to use the bar may be considered a major step forward in left-hand technique. Correct use of the bar makes the playing of certain chords and passages much easier; but incorrect placement can cause strain and tension in the left hand that is discouraging to beginners. The best plan, therefore, is to proceed gradually, using the minimum force neccessary and resting the hand at the first sign of strain.

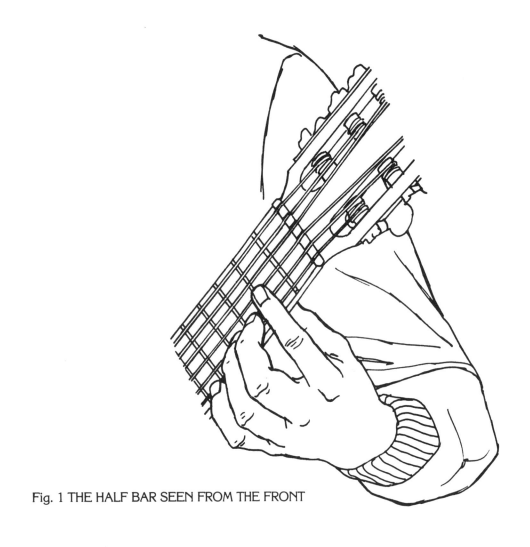

Fig. 1 THE HALF BAR SEEN FROM THE FRONT

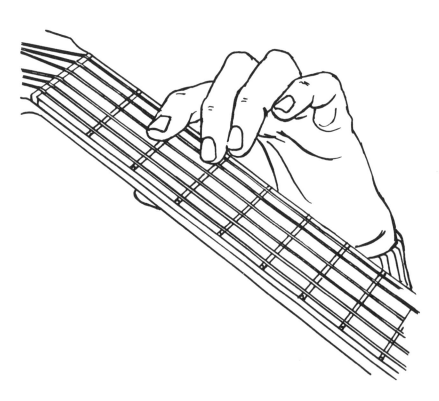

Fig. 2 THE HALF BAR FROM YOUR VIEWPOINT

The illustrations show a chord fingered with a half bar, and the way it is commonly written. Sometimes the letter C is used (an abbreviation for the word *capotasto,* which means "bar" in Italian): 1/2 CI, 1/2 CII, etc.

To play the chord, place the finger in the bar position as shown by the two diagrams. Press the strings just hard enough to ensure clear notes. This may be checked by first placing the half bar by itself, easing it down only until clarity is achieved. Then the second finger may be added to complete the chord.

Note that, although the example does not necessarily show the easiest way to finger that particular D chord, it becomes a distinct advantage in certain musical contexts where the lower notes are to be sustained:

Conventionally, the horizontal dotted line shows the duration of the half bar.

In the study below two new notes occur in measure 10 on the second string:

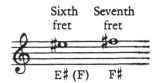

ANDANTINO Op. 241, No. 15   Ferdinando Carulli

MORE ABOUT CHORDS

The basic technique of chord playing was explained in Part I. It is time now to take a closer look at the right hand to ensure that chords can be played with the maximum sonority, volume, and clarity.

For a really clear sound, all the notes of the chord should be sounded exactly together, except when the chord is deliberately arpeggiated, as explained below. The secret of achieving this exactness lies in the preparation stage before the chord is actually played.

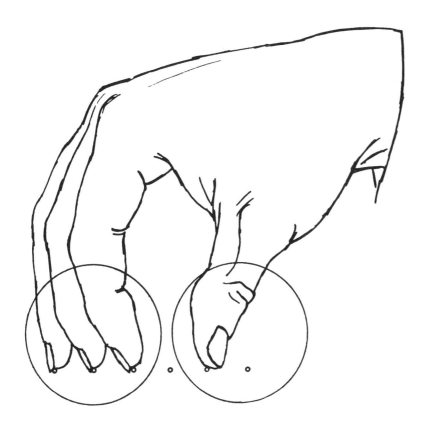

Fig. 3 THE PREPARATION POSITION FOR A FOUR NOTE CHORD

Study the diagram as a reminder of the basic technique and check the following points:

1. In the preparation stage, it should be possible to feel each of the strings in contact with the nails, except for the thumb, where the contact point is on the pad close to the nail. Without playing the chord, check this by squeezing the thumb and fingers toward each other enough to feel an even contact at all points.

2. When you feel balanced contact, you are ready to play the chord. This produces an even, controlled result and you will know in advance how the chord will sound. Snatching at a chord without preparation leaves too much to chance.

3. For a very loud chord, you may move the hand an inch or so towards the bridge; but playing too close to the bridge produces a harsh, grating sound. For very soft chords, try moving the hand more over the sound hole.

Try the following study, playing all the chords clearly and with all the notes together and distinct, so that each voice may be heard.

Exercise 2

Study in Chords

ARPEGGIATED CHORDS

Chords are sometimes played in a rippling style, with the notes being sounded not simultaneously but quickly one after the other from the lowest to the highest. This is not a simple arpeggio, where each of the notes is given a separate time value, but a chord arpeggiated so quickly that the notes are considered simultaneous in the way the chord is written. This is sometimes indicated by a zig-zag line beside the chord:

A less used alternative is:

The effect is exactly the same. Notice that the small notes have no actual time value and are simply used to give an idea of how the chord is played.

WHEN TO ARPEGGIATE

The rippling sound of arpeggiated chords has a pleasing effect when not done to excess. The habit of arpeggiating every chord must be avoided since this can become very irritating to the listener.

As a general rule, arpeggiation will be effective when the chord is followed by melody:

In contrast, a progression of chords sounds better played without arpeggiation:

In the study below, a suggested pattern of arpeggiation is marked.
However, remember that this is more often left to the taste of the player.

Chords of only two notes should rarely be arpeggiated, particularly when
several such chords occur in succession.

AMUSEMENT Op. 18, No. 3   Felix Horetzky (1800-1871)

SHORTHAND SYSTEMS FOR CHORDS

It is necessary to consider two simplified ways of writing chords, since these simplifications are used in many printed versions of songs, from traditional folk tunes to contemporary hits. The purpose of these systems is to give the guitarist a basic indication of harmony with which he can accompany the tune. For example, the first part of "On Top of Old Smokey" might be written thus:

The letter C indicates the chord of C major. A major chord consists of the first, third and fifth notes of the scale by the same name. In the case of C major, the notes are C, E, and G.

Components of a Major Chord

This system can be applied to find the notes of a major chord from any major scale. Notice that the C at the bottom of the chord is repeated (in musical terminology *doubled*) at the top. A C chord can be any number of Cs, Es, and Gs provided that there is at least one of each.

Let us look at the chord symbol which was provided in addition to the letter C.

The symbol represents the end of the guitar fingerboard closest to the nut, and the dots represent the fingertips placed on the strings. The numbers above show which finger plays on which string; the zeros indicate which open strings are to be played.

The complete notes of the chord symbol are

Notice that the C and E are doubled.

The Right Hand

A chord symbol only shows the placement of the left-hand fingers. It is up to the player to decide what to do with the right hand, which may play all the notes or only a few of them. For instance, the simplest way to play the chord would be to sweep with the thumb from the C up to the high E, thereby sounding all five possible notes. However, the following are all possible, and complete, C chords. They are complete because they all contain a C, and E, and a G.

Breaking up the Chords

The chord symbol does not indicate that all the notes must be played at once. One of the commonest forms of accompaniment uses the bass note (C) on the first beat and the rest of the chord on the remaining two beats:

Alternatively, the chord may be arpeggiated:

The main point to remember is that the chord symbols are only a guide for the left hand; what the right hand does depends on the imagination of the player.

Formation of More Complex Chords

The various rules for the formation of more complex chords are beyond the province of this book. However, there are many available chord books that illustrate with symbols the most commonly used combinations; and experimentation with printed music that includes chord symbols can be a useful and practical way to acquire a basic knowledge of harmony.

"On Top of Old Smokey" shows a simple interpretation of the chord symbols. Notice that changing the bass to one of the other notes of the chord adds variety and interest.

ON TOP OF OLD SMOKEY

EXPLORING NEW KEYS

Flat Keys

Flat keys are rare enough in guitar music to provide a welcome change of flavor when they are encountered. The scale of F major is given below, which together with the key of D minor (see page 00) has one flat in the key signature.

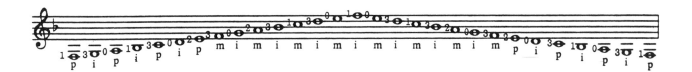

A suggested right-handed fingering is given which alternates p. and i. on the lower strings. In addition, the scale should be practiced using simple alternation with both i. and m. as the starting finger. When using simple alternation, take care that the right hand does not travel off position when playing the lower strings; there is a natural tendency to pull the hand back when moving from the higher to the lower strings.

Exercise 3

From the opera Jocelyn   Benjamin Godard (1849-1895)

STUDY IN F
Op. 31, No. 1

Fernando Sor (1778-1839)

Keys With More Sharps

One advantage that the guitar has, for instance, over the piano is that it is no more difficult to play in the key of E major with four sharps than in the key of C with no sharps at all. There are no black and white keys as on the piano, and one fret feels much the same as another.

In fact, the keys of A major and E major may be considered as "home keys" for the guitar, since they tend to make the most use of the open strings.

Working with a greater number of sharps in the key signature does require some effort to remember which notes are sharp, but if the key of D is now familiar, there is only one more sharp note to memorize for the key of A, which is G#.

Scale of A Major

In the simple form of the A major scale above, the first position is used as far as the third string. The remainder of the scale on the second and first strings uses the second position.

As before, the scale should be practiced using simple alternation in addition to the right-hand fingering suggested above.

Exercise 4

The St. Catherine   John Barrett (1674-1735)

ANDANTE from Op. 6   François Molino (1775-1847)

In this piece, give extra stress to the chords marked "Sf", the abbreviation for *Sforzando* which means "forcing."

ALMAN

Anon. (16th Century)

Scale of E Major

As with the A major scale, the first position is used for the lower four strings, then the second position for the remaining two. As well as the suggested fingering, simple alternation should be practiced, taking care to maintain a good right-hand position.

Exercise 5

Pastorale   F. N.

LITTLE RONDO A. Meissonier (b 1783)

m i a m i a m i m i m i m

cresc.

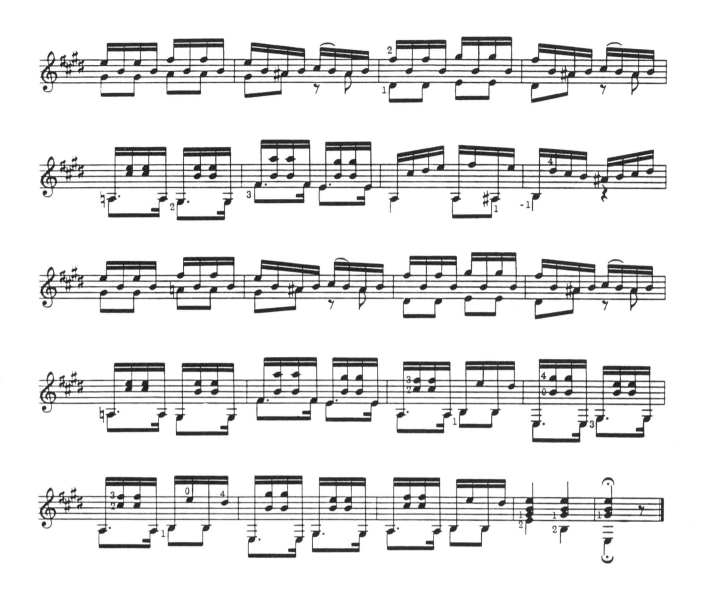

169

TECHNIQUE DEVELOPMENT

Movement in Thirds and Sixths

Simple two-note chords are often named by the interval between the notes.

The interval from C to D is called a *second*, from C to E a *third*, from C to F a *fourth*, etc.

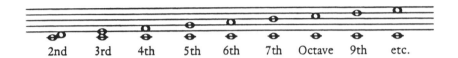

2nd   3rd   4th   5th   6th   7th   Octave   9th   etc.

I want to stress the importance of becoming used to successions of thirds and sixths, since these occur so frequently in the repertoire. The following two studies adapted from Fernando Sor's guitar method of 1830 are useful both for finger training and for developing familiarity with typical patterns.

Although the study in sixths is in broken form—that is one note of the chord sounded before the other—still the left hand should prepare *both* notes before either is played by the right hand. In fact, the study may be played first with both notes sounded simultaneously, and then, when the left-hand progressions become familiar, arpeggiated as written.

Exercise 6

Study in Sixths   Fernando Sor
(arranged F. N.)

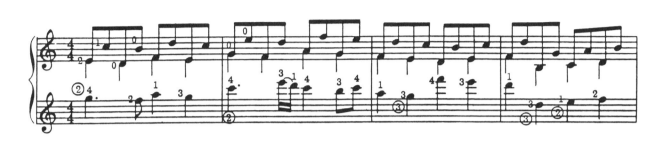

Fine

D. C. al Fine

Exercise 7

Study in Thirds

Fernando Sor
(arranged F. N.)

ALLEGRETTO Op. 44, No. 8   Fernando Sor

ANDANTINO Op. 139, No. 1 Mauro Giuliani (1781-1829)

MINOR SCALES

A minor scale shares a key signature with a major scale, to which it is said to be the related or *relative* minor. The relative minor of any major scale starts on the sixth note of the major scale. Thus the relative minor of C major is A minor, since A is the sixth note of the C major scale. The simplest form of the minor scale is known as the *natural minor.*

Natural Minor

The A minor scale shown above shares the key signature and notes of the C major scale. However, it does not include a note used when playing in the key of A minor: the G# used in the most common form of the phrase ending or *cadence.*

Cadence in A minor

This problem, which may be considered one of harmony, is solved in another form of minor scale known as the *harmonic minor.*

A minor, Harmonic form

Notice that the harmonic minor is the same as the natural minor except that the G is raised to G sharp for purposes of harmony. The drawback to the harmonic form is that it produces an awkward interval between the F and G#, which was once considered to be ugly and hard to sing. To produce a more singable, *melodic* minor scale, the F was sharped as well as the G in the ascending scale, thus avoiding the unmelodic interval. The descending scale simply follows the original form of the natural minor.

A minor, Melodic form

The melodic minor scale, which is the most complete form, is the one most often used in guitar instruction. Here are some examples of the melodic minor scales in the most used keys:

Melodic Minor Scales

Scale of D minor

Scale of A minor (two octaves)

Scale of E minor (two octaves)

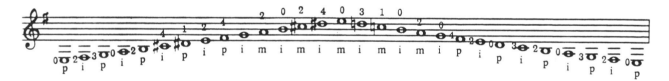

Practice these scales with simple alternation in addition to the fingerings suggested above.

Minor Chords

The minor chord in any key may be found by taking the first, third and fifth notes of the appropriate minor scale. For this purpose it does not matter which form of the minor scale is used, since these notes are common to all forms. The important difference between major and minor lies in the third note of the scale, which in minor chords is a half step lower.

Notes for the chord of A minor.

Common first position A minor chords.

STUDY IN D MINOR — Napoleon Coste (1806-1883)

In the second to last measure, the high chord can be found by a half bar at
the tenth fret as shown.

BOURREE IN A MINOR Leopold Mozart (1719-1787)

PETENERA Traditional

In this piece, each measure of 6/8 is followed by one of 3/4 time, a favorite
Spanish pattern.

SICILIENNE

Antoine Meissonier (b. 1783)

HOW TO GET THE MOST FROM YOUR MUSIC

If you have progressed this far you will almost certainly have discovered certain fundamental facts about the playing of music. One of the most important of these may be stated as follows:

It is Not Enough Just to Play The Notes.

Music is a language of subtlety and variety, and it is the way in which this language is used that reveals the fine musician. This is not say that such use can only be instinctive; there are specific ways to increase the interest and beauty of your playing that can be learned and practiced as a matter of technique. Some of the most obvious are:

1. The use of the full *dynamic* (loud and soft) range of the instrument.
2. The use of *tonal variety* to the fullest extent.
3. The observance of *correct tempo* and tempo changes.

Dynamics

The most common markings for loud and soft were given in Part II, page 51. In practice, many students ignore the indications completly or execute them in such a timid way that the difference between *fortissimo* and *pianissimo* is almost imperceptible. There are many reasons for this, but experience reveals that timidity, ranging from claims to a preference for soft sounds to a fear of revealing too much of oneself by being too expressive, is often the cause. Any music teacher can confirm that this attitude is not rare. And, the result is that the student's playing lacks variety and is boring. The guitar is in itself a quiet instrument, but it is essential to use its limited dynamic range to the fullest.

As a practical exercise, take any four-note chord and play it from the softest sound possible to the loudest consistent with hearing each of the notes and avoiding buzzes. At the soft end of the range, play more over the soundhole; for the very loud chords move the hand slightly closer to the bridge. Having established the full range clearly in your mind, try using this variety on pieces you already know. Naturally, not every piece calls for both extremes, but the experiment should be interesting and revealing.

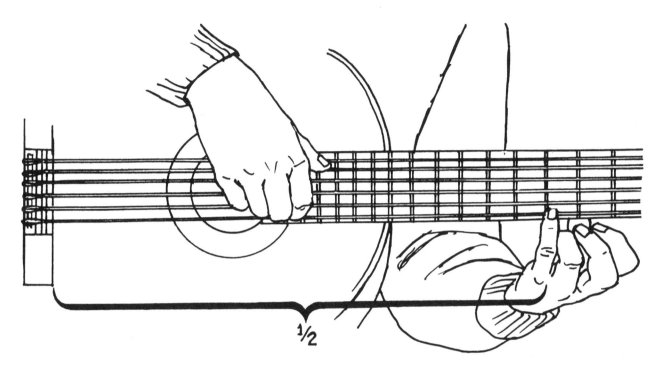

Fig. 4   THE ROUNDEST SOUND IS PRODUCED WHEN THE STRING
IS PLAYED AT THE HALF WAY POINT BETWEEN THE BRIDGE
AND THE FRET STOPPED BY THE LEFT HAND

Apart from the loud (forte) and soft (piano) and the gradual increase or decrease in sound (crescendo or diminuendo), there are other commonly used Italian terms related to dynamics:

Con brio—vigorously   Marcato—marked, accented
Energico—energetically   Perdendosi, Morendo—dying away
Leggiero—lightly   Sforzando—suddenly accented
Maestoso—majestically   Tranquillo—tranquil, gentle

Tonal Variety

The main device for tonal change on the guitar is similar to that used for dynamic change, that is the movement of the right hand more towards the bridge or more towards the soundhole.

A string produces its roundest sound when plucked at the halfway point between the fret, stopped by the left hand and the bridge. From there, as the right hand moves closer to the bridge, the sound becomes progressively more silvery or metallic in quality. However, there is more to it than simply moving the point at which the string is attacked. In general, the rest stroke is used to accentuate a round full note, with the free stroke used for the contrasting crystalline sound close to the bridge. Rest strokes close to the bridge tend to sound harsh and ugly; however, the free stroke must frequently be used when aiming for the rounder sound when chords or arpeggios make the use of the rest stroke impractical.

In practice, quite small movements of the hand in either direction can be made to yield a considerable variety of tone, and experimentation will reveal the many possibilities when the right-hand stroke is varied as well.

Vibrato

The left hand can contribute to tonal variety by using the technique known as "vibrato." With the appropriate finger in position on the string, the right hand plays the note while the left hand is moved quickly left and right along the same plane as the string. This has the effect of minutely raising and lowering the pitch of the tone. In general, too fast a movement produces a vibrato of exaggerated intensity; a relaxed and fluid movement is better.

Most students forget to continue the vibrato for the full value of the note. It takes practice to keep the movement going, but eventually this becomes a habit.

It is difficult to make a very noticeable vibrato at the first three frets. The effect becomes more pronounced when used on notes farther up the fingerboard. Also, the second string will be found more sensitive to vibrato than the first.

Vibrato at this fret on the first string is barely perceptible.

Vibrato at this point on the second string can be clearly audible and effective.

The abbreviation "vib" is sometimes encountered in the music, but more often the use of vibrato is left to the taste of the player. Other Italian terms associated with tonal variety are:

Cantabile—singing

Dolce—sweet

Espressivo—with expression

Metallico—metallic

Sul ponticello—near the bridge

The Importance of Tempo Markings

Instruction books tend to be full of recommendations to go slowly at first, and in general this is sound advice. However, when the preparatory stage is past, it is important to play a piece in its correct tempo. The most common fault is to play everything Andante.

We learned the most usual tempo markings in a Part II, page 44. The question is really what can be considered fast, as opposed to, for instance, fairly fast. Most metronomes have settings marked in the Italian terms as well as the numerical indication for the number of beats per minute; but the indications are usually more accurate for the piano or orchestra than for the guitar. It is unfortunately not physically possible to play a scale passage as fast on the guitar as on the piano or violin; hence the fastest markings must inevitably indicate a slower tempo for the guitar.

Rallentando

The term *rallentendo* (rall.) means becoming gradually slower. It is a characteristic of the final measure or two of a piece, since the slight slowing down is associated with finality. For this reason, it is important *not* to slow down if there is a repeat from the beginning before going to the end; the rallentando should be reserved for the very end only.

Other Changes in Tempo

The opposite of rallentando is *accelerando* (accel.). The effect is ended or cancelled by the indication "A tempo" (resume normal tempo). Other terms are *più mosso* (more quickly) and its oppostie *meno mosso* (less quickly) that indicate a specific change in tempo which is not gradual but immediate and which continues until counteracted by an instruction to return to the original tempo *(tempo primo)* or to go faster or slower. The following additional terms for tempo are in common use and should be memorized.

Ad libitum (ad lib.)—free, the speed at the choice of the player

Animato—animated, lively

Grave—very slow

Larghetto—a little faster than largo

Ritardando—coming gradually to a halt

Ritmico—rhythmically

Ritenuto—held back, suddenly slower

Vivace—very fast

Other Italian Terms

Some indications cannot be confined to the category of tempo, tone, or dynamics. A few examples are:

Appassionato—passionately

Brillante—brilliantly

Con brio—vigorously

Maestoso—majestically

Risoluto—boldly

Scherzando—playfully

Vivo—lively

All of these convey a mood which the player may interpret with a variety of means.

Here are a few more:

Molto—very, much

Più—more

Meno—less

Poco—a little

Quasi—almost

Sempre—Continuously

Ma non troppo—but not too much

Conclusion

Composers have many ways to indicate how they want their music to sound. In addition to the basic indications of notes and tempo, there are the more subtle gradings of dynamics, rhythm, and mood. A good player will be sensitive to these indications in the score so as to interpret as faithfully as possible the original conception of the composer.

The following extract from a Sonatina by Giuliani has been chosen to give the opportunity of interpreting a more extended work. I have suggested a number of dynamic and other markings for extra practice in this area.

RONDO from the Sonatina, Op. 71   Mauro Giuliani (1781-1829)

SELF TEST

This test is from all three parts of the first course. Many students find it useful to check their progress up to this point in order to discover and strengthen any weak areas before going on to the next stage.

1.   Name and play each of these notes:

2.   Name the major keys which have these signatures:

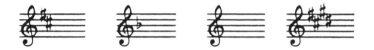

3.   Fill in the missing rests:

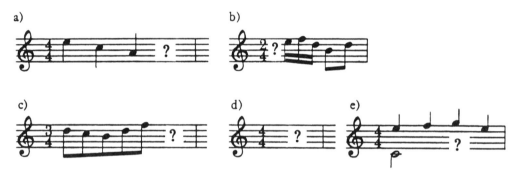

4.   Name the minor keys which have these signatures:

5.   Arrange these Italian tempo terms in order from slow to fast: Moderato, Allegro, Lento, Presto, Allegretto, Adagio, Largo.

6.   Arrange these dynamic indications in order from softest to loudest:

ff, *mp*, *mf*, *pp*, *f*, *p*.

7.   Define the following terms: Arpeggio, free stroke, whole tone, tetrachord, duet, slur, postion, alternation, damping, grace note.

8. Identify what is incorrectly written in the following examples:

9. Write in the melodic minor scale of D (one octave):

10. Insert bar lines to make complete measures:

11. Explain the meaning of the following:

    Allegro ma non troppo
    Ad Lib.
    Più lento
    Scherzando
    Con brio

12. Play at sight the following:

GOING ON FROM HERE

If you have successfully completed this stage, the next step will be to learn the upper positions of the fingerboard, the full bar, and the various ways by which technique can be advanced to embrace a more challenging repertoire. Two more of my advanced instruction books are available: *Solo Guitar Playing,* Volumes I and II. I have also prepared a series of anthologies by musical period entitled Renaissance, Baroque, and Classical guitar. Each of these contains pieces graded from easy to moderately difficult, with a background of the musical period and study notes to assist with the difficult passages.

One of the best ways to expand knowledge of the repertoire is to collect records. The best players can thus be heard, and the student will have the opportunity to define his own taste and area of interest.

The help of a knowledgeable teacher is of course invaluable and must be recommended. In addition, some music shops have musicians on their staff who will help in the location of favorite pieces and give general advice.

One of the joys of the guitar is that there is always more: more to learn, more ways to produce a beautiful sound, and more rewards with each step of progress. It is hoped that these books will have helped to start a pleasant journey that for some will last a lifetime.